Lore
of
The River

Lore of the River
The Shoals of Long Ago

-An Early History
-Of the Muscle Shoals
-Legends of the River
-Its Earliest People
-Sketches of Some Noble Chiefs
-Arrival of the First White Settlers

- Expanded 3rd Edition -
2007

By Dr. William Lindsey McDonald

Bluewater Publications, U.S.A.

Lore of the River

Published by
Bluewater Publications
Formerly known as: Heart of Dixie Publishing Co.

For all of your publishing needs, visit our website:
www.BluewaterPublications.com

DEDICATION

This book is dedicated to my great-grandson,
Mark Alloway Middleton, who was born
February 24, 2003. Just in time to meet
the publication date for this revised edition
of *Lore of The River*.

*"In the face of a new generation, I am assured that my
yesterdays have not been wasted, and that my
tomorrows have been joyfully renewed in a journey
that never ends."*

RECOGNITION

In Recognition of my dear friend of many
years, the late, James Jackson of Memphis,
Tennessee; he assisted in the funding of
the first publication in 1989.

James Jackson, was a native of Tuscumbia, Alabama. He was a
direct descendant of James Jackson, an early settler of the
Muscle Shoals on the Tennessee River, one of the original
founders of the City of Florence, Alabama, and builder of the
Forks of Cypress, an early landmark of Lauderdale County.

James Jackson died in 1995 at the age of 99. A
memorial service was held for him by the author
at the Forks of Cypress Cemetery, Florence,
Alabama, September 14, 1995.

FOREWORD

The archives and legends that tell of the past make Chief Doublehead's life and death seem fictional. The stories of Chiefs Colbert and Tuscumbia of the Chickasaws, and the brief escapades of the Creek Warrior Big Foot lend more wonder and romance to the personalities that make up the lore of Muscle Shoals.

But this book commences many centuries before that era when the white man first began his explorations of Northwest Alabama. The knowledge that people lived in the Tennessee Valley for over thousands of years becomes one of the most remarkable chapters of the history of the area.

These events of early man are portrayed on the banks of a river that, according to the geographers and geologists, probably did not flow through the most Northern and western part of Alabama in the early dawn of time.

These tales of people and places, battles, tragedy, and the struggles of long ago, are a vital part of the story of the River and the Shoals.

- the author

Mound, with maple tree on top

FLORENCE UNDER THE HILL – Probably a thousand years before the establishment of Florence in 1818 at the top of the hill, there was a thriving community at the bottom of the hill. This ancient ceremonial mound, called "Wawmanona" by the Indians, was built sometime between 100 B.C. and 400 A.D. and served as the center of this early town that predated Florence. This 1890 view shows the mound, in the backyard. (A lonely Maple Tree once stood on top of the mound.)

Table of Contents

These sketches of early Native Americans at the Shoals are from the canvas of Dorothy Carter McDonald.

A view of how the Tennessee River looked prior to the completion of Wheeler Dam in 1936.

One of the early water-powered
grist mills at the Muscle Shoals.
The site of this mill is now covered
by beautiful Wilson Lake.

1 THE COURSE OF THE TENNESSEE RIVER

Photograph of the Muscle Shoals prior to the building of Wilson Dam.

The serpentine course of the Tennessee River from where it begins at the confluence of the Holston and French Broad Rivers near Knoxville, Tennessee, to where it empties into the Ohio River near Paducah, Kentucky, has raised questions from the very earliest days. Why it runs southwestward, then northwestward, and, finally, northward, remains a matter of conjecture, and probably always will as long as man studies its path and wonders about its origin.

Numerous theories have been advanced by geographers and geologists. One involves the hypothetical "Appalachian River" that flowed from its source near Knoxville in a Southwestern direction all the way to the Gulf of Mexico without turning to the North and west, as does the present Tennessee.

Another theory contends that out of the westward slopes of the Cumberland's flowed a stream, which held a western course, similar to that part of the present Tennessee that passes through the Northern part of the state of Alabama. This ancient stream, according to conjecture, flowed southwestward into the Mississippi River system. It is further supposed that a Northward flowing tributary of the Ohio River was stimulated by deformations in the earth's surface that diverted the westward flowing stream into the Northward flowing waters that joined the Ohio.

There is yet another theory, based on the geological deposits evidencing old river channels. From such deposits in Alabama it seems probable that the ancestral Tennessee was the major stream of the system flowing through the region. It is indicated that the mouth of this stream shifted laterally from time to time, and retreated Northeastward as the land in the Northeastern part of the State of Alabama sank, allowing an ancient sea to advance to within a short distance of Walden Gorge. When this primeval sea retreated and the Southern Appalachian region was left warped and elevated, the Tennessee River took the course it now follows west of Chattanooga through the gorge.

Most all of these theories tell us that at some point in time what is now the Tennessee River was not a part of the familiar topography of Northwest Alabama.

As the wandering Tennessee made its way across North Alabama in search of its new route to the Gulf, it readily cut through what was generally the limestone of the Cumberland Plateau formation. Thus, it created a normal bed, in width and depth, for its permanent course until it reached the North-western part of the State of Alabama.

As it approached the area that was to become known as the Muscle Shoals, the river made its way across a fall line. Normally, the coastal fall lines occur within a hundred miles or so of the sea. This fall line is close to 400 miles from the Gulf of Mexico. However, it was much nearer to a sea dating from a period of great age that, according to some sources, covered that section of Alabama where the city of Birmingham is located.

In a distance of some 37 miles the fall line at the Muscle Shoals dropped a distance of about 137 feet. Had this been a sudden drop the fall would have appeared as a small Niagara, where the lowest part of this spectacular tourist site measures around 160 feet.

The Muscle Shoals on the Tennessee in Northwest Alabama was a serious obstruction on the river, creating, for all practical purposes, two rivers, the Upper and the Lower Tennessee's. The water rushing over these shoals formed cataracts, pools, reefs, sandbars, numerous islands shallows and swift and rushing currents.

The Federal Government attempted to channel around these shoals on the river in the early part of the 19th Century, but it was never really completed. A second and more successful effort was made in the later part of that century. It was not until the building of Wilson Dam in the early part of the 20th Century, and the advent of the Tennessee Valley Authority in 1933, that these hazardous, and sometimes terrifying, shoals were finally and completely conquered by the engineering genius of man.

Another unusual feature of the river at the Muscle Shoals was the width of its bed. It resembled some parts of the mighty Mississippi as it made its way across the shallow rapids.

Wilson Dam completed in 1925. Picture shows elevated spillage of waters in the spill ways from Wilson Lake due to heavy rains.

Downriver from the Muscle Shoals, at the Mississippi line, where the river turns to flow Northward, it follows the strike of cretaceous rock formations left by a primordial sea which are easily eroded and through which the river could readily cut a normal course.

The rapids of the Muscle Shoals in Northwest Alabama became in time a natural habitat for a fresh water mussel fauna that gave its name to the Muscle Shoals.

There is evidence of mussel harvesting that goes back to the very earliest peoples who came to this section of the Southeast.

4

The mussel was easily available year round, and became a basic food staple that enabled prehistoric Indians to build their permanent camps at the Muscle Shoals thousands of years ago.

The history of the people at the Muscle Shoals is also the story of the great Tennessee River. Its presence in Northwest Alabama has been the resource that provided the prosperity that has made the Muscle Shoals a wonderful and beautiful place for man to make his home.

2 THE ANCIENT INDIANS

Excavations at the Standfield-Worley Shelter in Colbert County, Alabama.

PREHISTORIC PEOPLE AT THE SHOALS

The earliest people to arrive at the Muscle Shoals are known as the late Paleo tradition. Their life and behavior were reminiscent of Old World Upper Paleolithic cultures, which had spread across Central Asia all the way to Japan. It is widely accepted that the earliest Americans came out of Siberia and across the Bering Strait into Alaska during the last advance of the Ice Age, when climatic conditions similar to those prevailing today began to occur.

These late Paleo tribesmen were nomadic wanderers, moving about as the seasons changed. They usually lived in closely-knit bands of from 20 to 40 members. Such groups perhaps included a grandfather, his sons, grown grandsons, and their families. They most often held kinship ties with nearby groups.

Some two thousand years later, a new tradition, called the Archaic People, began to take shape in the Eastern United States. Their way of life was more complex, and perhaps became the first to permanently inhabit the Muscle Shoals. The Archaic tradition probably developed gradually from the older and more primitive Paleo culture.

These people of the Archaic tradition first made their homes under rock shelters and in caves. Later, they often built camp-sites on shell mounds, and, hence, became known locally as the Shell Mound Indians. Eventually they learned the art of cooking through a process of dropping heated rocks into food that had been placed in hollowed-out depressions in stone or in their hard-packed floors. They developed an art of weaving and how better to make tools and weapons than by using bones as well as stones.

Abundance of year-around food supplies, plus a more moderate weather, was what brought these ancient peoples to this part of the South. The shallows and rapids at the Muscle Shoals was a natural habitat for the small freshwater shellfish called the mussel. These little morsels of meat, which gave their name to this section of the Tennessee River, could be scooped up and eaten the year around. This presented a dependable staple rarely found in other parts of the country.

In the nearby hardwood forests could be found nuts, roots, berries and all kinds of game, large and small. Some archeologists think that the Tennessee Valley was, perhaps, the most heavily populated area in the Southeast at one time or another during the ancient past.

Overhanging rock shelters, limestone caves, and old shell mounds continue to unlock long-hidden evidences of the presence of early man at the Muscle Shoals. A few skeletal remains found in the Standfield-Worley Shelter in Colbert County indicate that the earliest arrivals at the Shoals were not much different in size and height than the people who live here today. One male was five feet and nine inches in height; a female skeleton measured five feet and one inch.

A fishhook excavated from Dust Cave – located a few miles west of Florence – is believed to be the earliest ever found in Alabama. This rare artifact indicates that there were fishermen along the Tennessee River long before the building of the pyramids in Egypt and the founding of the ancient cities of Europe, Asia, and Asia Minor.

THE EARLIEST FARMERS AT THE SHOALS

The first farmers at the Muscle Shoals were a prehistoric people identified by archaeologists as those of the Woodland tradition. They followed a hunting and gathering way of life similar to that of their ancestors, the late Paleo and Archaic peoples. Yet, they established more refinements and better efficiencies in securing and storing food. They had the advantage of the bow and arrow which gave them more skill in warfare and hunting. Their civilization saw the beginning of elementary agriculture as they learned how to plant seeds and to care for growing plants. They developed a primitive industry of making pottery that became locally stylized in form and decoration. Burial customs, which were gaining importance during the earlier

Archaic tradition, were followed in the Woodland culture by elaborate burials of certain individuals. Many of their mounds were constructed over human bones or cremated remains, or in some cases, the mounds were built over log tombs.

The Woodland people were inhabitants of the Muscle Shoals from approximately 2,000 B.C. until around 800 A.D. They built their homes in small settlements, which were more permanent than those of their ancestors. Yet, they found it necessary to relocate their small communities from time to time in search of better and more available food resources.

It was during this prehistoric Woodland period when the Copena culture appeared at the Shoals. Copena is a Southern form of the Hopewell culture identified with the Ohio Valley that spread along the western edge of the Appalachian Mountains. This shaping of a higher form of civilization is believed to have originated in Illinois and Ohio. This term comes from their use of copper and galena, which is a crude form of lead ore.

Nearby Savannah, Tennessee, seems to have been the local center of the Copena tradition. Its influence ascended the Tennessee River where its artifacts can be identified with a number of sites around Waterloo, Wright, Smithsonia, and Florence. Prior to the impoundment of Pickwick Lake in 1938, many of the mounds, villages, and camp sites that were to be flooded were carefully studied. Some of those that were excavated offered excellent evidence of the Copena culture.

These ancient Woodland and Copena people were the original mound builders in this area. Their earthworks varied in both form and function. Some were only a few feet high while others were more immense.

There is evidence that The Florence Mound was probably built during the Woodland period between 100 B.C. and 400 A.D. This mound is perhaps the oldest man-made structure in this area. Its antiquity identifies the site of Florence as having been occupied by a pre-historic people at or near the time its namesake, Florence, Italy, was being rebuilt by the veterans of the Roman General Sulla a few years after his return from Asia Minor in 83 B.C.

THE PRE-HISTORIC MISSISSIPPIAN PEOPLE

For more than 900 years, from about A.D. 800 until around A.D. 1500, the Muscle Shoals was the home of a prehistoric people known as the Mississippians. Their more advanced culture began taking shape between A.D. 700 and 800 on the Mississippi River between present day St. Louis, Missouri, and Vicksburg, Mississippi. From there it spread in all directions, mainly along river systems in most parts of the Southeast. By about A.D. 1200, their social groups in what is now Southern Illinois, Southwestern Indiana, Eastern Missouri, Western Kentucky, Northeastern Arkansas, most of Tennessee, Northern Mississippi, and Northern Alabama, had developed the highest cultural advancement in all of North America.

Hunting and gathering, as with their ancestors, continued to be a significant source of their livelihood. They relied heavily on agriculture, especially in the cultivation of beans, squash, and a new variety of corn that is believed to have been domesticated in the highlands of Guatemala. Their main farming tools were a digging stick and a short-handle hoe with a blade made of chipped flint or the bones of large animals.

What was new in this advanced civilization was that they developed a more centralized political structure. This led to more powerful leaders and a stronger military defense capability for their cities.

The Mississippians are sometimes called "Mound Builders." Their style of mounds were usually flat-topped with steep sides. These mounds served as platforms for religious temples and houses for chiefs or for other important functions. They shared religious beliefs which involved similar ceremonial costumes, ritual objects, and religious symbols.

Every island of any size at the Muscle Shoals was crowded with their mounds and villages. Sometimes referred to locally as "The Koger Island People," their center was on Koger and Seven Mile Islands located a few miles downriver from the Muscle Shoals. Smaller villages could be found along the nearby rivers and creeks.

More than seventy mounds in the immediate area of the Muscle Shoals can be identified on maps that were drawn before the coming of Wilson, Wheeler, and Pickwick Dams. In the Pickwick Basin, alone, there were more than forty mounds and at least 150 villages and camp sites. Most of these are identified with the Mississippi Culture, although a number were of the earlier Woodland and Copena period. Although there is evidence to show that the Florence Mound was probably constructed earlier than the Mississippian age, it is believed to have served the "Koger Island People" as their center of worship, or "holy ground."

Almost one and one-half centuries passed between the age of the great Mississippian Culture and the presence of the historic Indians who were at the Muscle Shoals when the first white settlers arrived. When questioned about the presence of these mounds along the Tennessee River, the Creek, Cherokee, and

Chickasaw Indians did not seem to know about their purpose, how they were built, or who were the builders of these ancient temples.

THE FLORENCE MOUND, AN ANCIENT CATHEDRAL

The Indian Mound at Florence was somewhat of a mystery even to the Native Americans at the Muscle Shoals when the first white settlers arrived and began to ask questions. These Historic Indians knew little about its age, its builders, or its purpose. The mound stands today as a shrine shrouded by an ancient aura that continues to baffle all attempts to define its reason for being and its true place in the history of a forgotten people.

This temple mound is a monument not only to the compelling power of a religion but also to the leadership of the community of believers responsible for its construction. It points to the genius of an early man, whether chieftain or high priest. Although its basic concept was borrowed from an even more ancient culture, its construction at the Shoals came into being as a result of a conceived plan that dictated its location and structured the labor forces that were employed in it fabrication.

There were actually three mounds at this location when the first white settlers arrived; the existing mound is the only one that has survived. The other two were nearby and were smaller in size, their heights estimated to have been about 25 feet. These three mounds below Florence were once partly enclosed by an oblong shaped earthen wall beginning on the downstream side about 600 to 800 feet from the existing mound and bordering the mounds to a point on the upstream side. It is possible that surrounding these mounds and earthen wall complex was a moat that connected with the river.

The earthen wall was thought to have been from twelve to fifteen feet in height. Prior to the Civil War a historian noted that the wall had been cultivated until it was difficult to trace except during the times it was being plowed. Then, he said, one could distinguish the yellow clay of which the wall was composed from the dark sand of the surrounding area. Also, parts of this earthen wall were used as land fill for the railroad beds on the North bank of the river more than a hundred years ago.

The immensity of the Florence Mound is almost overwhelming when one considers the methods used in its construction. This quadrilateral mound, the largest mound on the Tennessee River, stands forty-three feet in height. Its base measurements are 310 feet by 230 feet. It has a distinctive flat top that is 145 feet in length and ninety-four feet in width.

Limited research conducted by the University of Alabama in May, 1996, unearthed evidence to indicate that this mound was probably built during the Woodland Tradition between 100 B.C. and 400 A.D. This is about 1,000 years earlier than had previously been estimated by archaeologists. Without question, the Florence Mound is the oldest man-made structure at Florence.

During De Soto's explorations in the New World around 1540 his people observed a mound actually being constructed. Dirt, they said, was carried up in one basket at a time, emptied out, and then stamped down with great force until it had the desired consistency. Perhaps this represents a near description of how the local earthen structure was erected, although the Florence Mound was built much earlier.

The Woodland Tradition emerged as a distinctive culture of people in the eastern states, especially along the Ohio and

Mississippi rivers. This involved changes in their lifestyle. It also brought about a marked innovation in the ideology of its population.

It is believed that the Woodland People built the Florence Mound as a place of worship. One of the two nearby smaller mounds - no longer existing - perhaps was used as a base for the house where the high priest or chief resided. The second smaller mound

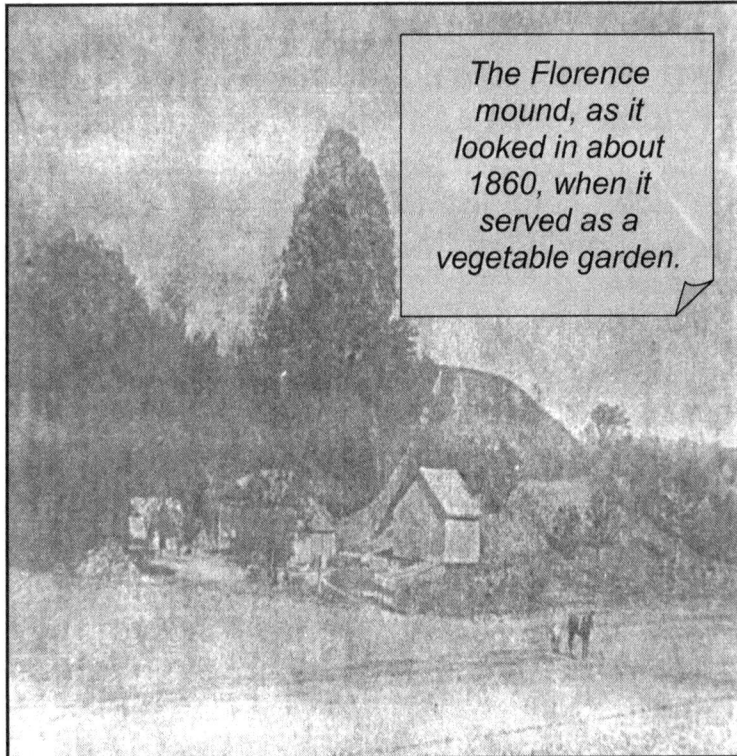

The Florence mound, as it looked in about 1860, when it served as a vegetable garden.

may have been for the secondary priests or chiefs. It is also possible that it served as the base for a mortuary where the dead were prepared for burial. However, the existing ceremonial Florence Mound contains no burials, based upon excavations that were made in 1914.

During these examinations, evidence was found in an adjacent field suggesting that a habitation area was once associated with the mound. Some think that a large portion, if not all, of the Muscle Shoals area was regarded by these early people as their "holy ground." Generally, this part of the Shoals was not used for dwellings or towns. Perhaps the priestly hierarchy lived

15

on the grounds outside the wall surrounding the Florence Mound.

The sides of the mound were purposely built so steep that it was difficult for man to climb them. Thus, the entrance to the small wooden temple at the top, where a sacred fire burned, had to be made up the wide steps constructed of logs and dirt on the eastern slope. Here ascended the priests, or perhaps the high priest, in magnificent regalia to greet the rising sun to the east and to call for blessings upon the people and the land.

There were special holy days and seasons of celebrations in which the Florence Mound was used as a great cathedral for a mysterious people who made religion the center of their civilization for hundreds of years at the Muscle Shoals. It is a monument to the religion of an ancient people.

Some two miles below the Florence Mound is an archaeological site believed to have been the dwelling place of a people more ancient than those of the Woodland period. Here, human bones have laid in the earth so long that they have gone through a state of petrifaction. Thus, when one looks below the hill where rests the modern city of Florence, he becomes aware that ancient man established his home here thousands of years before the arrival of the Europeans.

Sometime around 1400, well before the arrival of the Europeans, the great Mississippi Culture began to decline. These Mound Builders did not disappear, but their structured, centralized societies broke down. The centers were gradually abandoned, and most of the Mississippian peoples returned to a simpler way of life. A number of sources believe that the broad Mississippian Culture broke up into smaller tribes such as the historic Cherokees and Chickasaws of the Muscle Shoals area.

Circa 1900

The first white settlers in the area reported, however, that the Indians they encountered appeared to know nothing about the earlier people who had built the great mounds in the Tennessee Valley.

The Florence Mound remains in many ways a mystery. It stands in the Twenty First Century as one of the few architectural features of an advanced civilization that at one time called the Muscle Shoals their home.

For the next 200 years or more after the decline of the ancient Mississippi Culture, the Muscle Shoals area became practically uninhabited. This area was claimed as a part of the sacred hunting grounds of a number of tribes that were a part of the Historic Culture who were in the area when the white settlers arrived the Chickasaws, Creeks, and Cherokees. In one instance involving negotiations with the Henderson Land Company in 1774, the Chickasaws refused to permit the white men to go near the mouth of Occochapo, their name for Bear Creek.

An artist's conjectural painting of the Indian Mound about 100 B.C., showing the temple on the flat top, and the steps leading up the east slope (A pastel by Dorothy Carter McDonald, loaned by the Indian Mound Museum, Florence, Alabama.)

Negotiations that would eventually take away the Indian claims to the Muscle Shoals began as early as 1798. Finally, after the 1816 Treaty, most of the land was ceded to the United States Government and the white settlers began to move in. The last of the Native Americans were evicted in 1837 and 1838. Their descendants in the Red River Valley of Oklahoma still refer to their ancestral home at the Muscle Shoals as "a good land".

3 HISTORIC INDIANS

Painting by Dorothy Carter McDonald
(Courtesy of the Florence Indian Mound Museum)

THE EARLY INDIANS IN ALABAMA

The term "Historic Indians" identifies the Native Americans who were met by the white settlers. In general, the Historic Indians knew little or nothing about their predecessors. There were exceptions, of course. When the young Frenchman, Le Clere Milfort, visited the Creeks on the Chattahoochee River in 1776, he was impressed with their system of preserving the stories of their ancestors.

The old men exhibited to him strands of pearls which were used as archives. The arrangement of the pearls on the display represented principal events of the past. These symbols enabled the Creek historian to tell stories of their ancestors.

The Historic Indians living in Alabama during the time Hernando De Soto made his way through the state in 1542 were:

- The Coosas, whose territory embraced the present counties of Benton, Talledega, Coosa, and a portion of Cherokee County.
- The Tallases who lived upon the Tallaposa and its tributary streams.
- The Mobilians whose lands fell between what is now the cities of Montgomery and Mobile.
- The Choctaws inhabited Green, Marengo, Tuscaloosa, Sumpter and Pickens Counties in Alabama as well as a part of the adjoining state of Mississippi.
- The Alabamas who lived on the Tombigbee and Alabama Rivers and, later, at the junction of the Coosa and Tallapoosa.
- The Chickasaws who occupied a portion of Northwest Alabama, Northern Mississippi, Eastern Tennessee and the Southwest corner of Kentucky.
- The Cherokees who had towns extending from Tennessee and Northwest Georgia into the upper regions of Alabama.

- The Yuchi people were at the Muscle Shoals at the time De Sota crossed into eastern Alabama. The Yuchi were later evicted by the war-like Shawnee.

THE ALABAMAS

Alabama received its name from the small tribe of the Alabamas who were also known as Aibamus and Alabamons. These people migrated into Alabama during the 1500's from Northeast Mississippi and stayed around for 200 years. They first occupied the land near the junction of the Tombigbee and Alabama Rivers.

Around 1600, they moved up the Alabama River to the vicinity of present day Selma and, again, some 80 years later, to the junction of the Coosa and Tallapoosa Rivers. Around the end of the 17th Century it is said that they had only about 150 warriors. During the French occupation of Fort Toulouse it was estimated that the population of the Alabama tribe was around 4,500 men, women and children.

THE CHOCTAWS

In 1771 the number of Choctaw warriors was shown as 2,340 in the records at Mobile, Alabama. The eastern district of their nation was known as Oy-pat-oo-coo-la, meaning "small nation". The western part included the districts, or towns, of Oo-coo-la, Falaya, Hanete and Chickasaha.

According to tradition, they and the Chickasaws descended from a people called the Chickemicaws, who were among the first inhabitants of the Mexican empire.

Since the Choctaws formed the heads of their infants into different shapes by compression, they were called "flat heads".

The men were raw-boned and extremely active. The features of the female were described as "lively and agreeable".

The males dressed similar to that of the Creeks. Their styles were influenced by their wealth or poverty. However, they all wore a flap made of buckskin. The female usually wore only a petticoat reaching from the waist to the knees, while some of the richer classes wore a covering on the neck and shoulders.

The Choctaws were superior orators who spoke with good sense, using beautiful metaphors. Their speeches were concise, strong and full of fire. It has been recorded that the Choctaw warriors were timid in war when fighting at other places, but fought like desperate veterans when their homes came under attack.

THE CREEK NATION

The definition of the Creek Nation is a confederacy of peoples chiefly of Muskogean stock formerly occupying most of Alabama and Georgia and parts of Florida.

These people at one time claimed the area in and around the Muscle Shoals. Even during the late 18th Century a few of their clansmen, including the notable Chief Big Foot, were residing in the area of present day Colbert and Lauderdale Counties.

Their color was the same as one would see on the 21st Century Indian Reservations in the west. The males were admirably proportioned, athletic, and graceful in their movements. Generally, they were taller than the Europeans, some standing more than six feet in height.

The females were smaller, and many of them, according to early documents, were beautiful. Corpulence was rare. However, it is said that one chief who lived across the Florida line was so fat that he was compelled to move about his house upon his hands and knees.

Both sexes adorned themselves with ornaments, consisting of pretty shells and fresh water pearls, while the better classes wore moccasins and buskins of dressed deer leather.

When the Creeks were victorious in battle, they mutilated the enemies' bodies in the most brutal manner. The arms and legs were cut around, and then severed from the body by blows upon the bone. The head was cut around just above the ears, and the whole scalp jerked off. These were then quickly smoked over a fire and borne off in triumph to their homes, with the arms and legs suspended upon their spears.

THE YUCHI WERE EARLY RESIDENTS AT THE SHOALS

In the language of the American archaeologists and historian, the term, "prehistoric people," is used to identify the earliest of the human race who were in America before the arrival of the first explorers and adventurers from the Old World.

Those tribes who were later encountered by these explorers and the colonists who arrived in America are known as the "Historic Indians." These historic Indians, with exceptions of a few individuals who lived among them, were inarticulate; hence, the records of their history were written by the white man.

In Alabama this watershed for Native American history centers around the year 1540 when the Spanish explorer, Hernando De

Soto, crossed the Blue Ridge Mountains and reached the upper part of the Coosa River in Northeast Alabama.

The first known tribe of historic Indians to make the Muscle Shoals their home was known as the Yuchi. It is believed that, perhaps, they had been in Northwest Alabama for quite some time before De Soto's encounter with them among the Upper Creek Indians in Northeast Alabama in July, 1540.

Little is known about the Yuchi, who called themselves "children of the sun." They were sometimes referred to as the Tohogalega, or Hogaloge. A number of early maps refer to the upper Tennessee River as the "Thegalego," and the lower part as the "Hogalegee." Both of these names were variations of spellings used for early peoples who lived along the shores of the Tennessee River.

The Yuchi moved often, and although they became a part of the Creek Confederacy they did not mix well with other tribesmen. In fact, they were not well liked by the other Southern Indians. This may have been partly because their language was entirely confusing to other Indians in the Southeast, and by their refusal to learn other dialects.

Some anthropologists think that the Yuchi were an isolated fragment of the Siouans who were, as far as is known, the earliest historic Indians in the South. The Siouans had broken away from a Northern people who lived in the area of the Great Lakes before the time of Christopher Columbus. As they migrated Southward, one of their splinter groups, the Yuchi, reached the Tennessee River to claim the Muscle Shoals as their home.

The Siouans and Yuchi had an unusual custom of flattening the heads of their children. They practiced body tattooing. Most of their rituals centered around the worship of the sun.

They were tall, light-skinned, had long hair and, strangely enough, were reported to have had blue-eyes. Their women were noted for their beauty, and were sought after as wives.

After leaving the Muscle Shoals, these people of the North, the Yuchi, became a part of the Creek Federation, although they continued to maintain a pride in their own customs and rituals.

The first of the Yuchi to move west was in 1829 as part of the Lower Creek Nation. Their final movement in the Trail of Tears was in 1836 when they left Alabama with the main group of Creeks.

WHEN THE SHAWNEE PEOPLE LIVED AT THE SHOALS

Almost lost among the hundreds of years of unrecorded history of North Alabama is the story of the Shawnees. It was these war-like people who ousted the Yuchi to become the second group of historic Indians to make their home in the Muscle Shoals area.

These Algonkian-speaking Shawnees are thought to have descended from a particular stage of advancement in Native American civilization called the Fort Ancient Culture. The Fort Ancient, in turn, had been influenced by the earlier mound builders of the Middle Mississippian Period whose territory once extended all the way from Southern Wisconsin to the middle part of Alabama. The Fort Ancient Culture existed from about A.D. 1400 to approximately A.D. 1650 in an area that covered

Northeastern Kentucky, Southern Ohio, and western West Virginia.

The Shawnees lived in the central Ohio Valley until the 17th century when they were driven out by the Iroquois and scattered into widely separated areas. Some settled in what is now Illinois. One group was forced Southward into the Cumberland Valley near present Nashville. Another band moved to the Southeast to the Savannah River in South Carolina and Georgia. It was during this time that they were first called Shawnee, a name derived from an Algonkian word meaning "South" or "Southerners." The Alabama Creeks and early white settlers referred to them as "Savannahs" because they once lived along the Savannah River.

During the spring and summer months the Shawnees lived in bark-covered houses grouped into rather large villages. Each village had a council house which was also used for religious ceremonies. Among these celebrated events were the Spring and Autumn Bread Dance, the Green Corn Dance, and the Purification Ceremony for warriors.

The village women planted and cultivated corn and other crops in the fields that were almost always located in the rich bottom lands that had been cleared for agricultural purposes along creeks and rivers. These villages were usually abandoned during the fall and winter seasons when small family groups realigned themselves into hunting camps.

It was the Shawnee group along the Cumberland River who ousted the Yuchi from the Muscle Shoals. It is not known how long the Shawnees lived in North Alabama, perhaps a century or more. However, in 1715, at the beginning of the twelve-year Creek and Cherokee War, the Cherokee Indians, with the aid of their Chickasaw neighbors, expelled the Shawnees from along the Red River in Kentucky.

After 1725, the scattered Shawnees united again in the region of Ohio, where they formed the principal barrier to the advance of white settlers. They produced one of the great Native American warrior-statesman, Tecumseh, who tried, but failed, to unify the other Southern Indians against the United States.

The total Shawnee population perhaps ranged from 2,000 to 3,000 during historic times. In 1960, their three main settlements in Oklahoma numbered about 2,250 people.

THE CHEROKEES

There were a few Cherokee villages at the Muscle Shoals when the first white settlers arrived. One of their minor chiefs, Doublehead, made his home at various locations, at Colbert County near Cherokee, in Limestone County, near Brown's Ferry, and in Lauderdale County near The Forks of Big Cypress and Little Cypress Creeks and near the mouth of Blue Water Creek.

North Alabama was the Southwestern tip of their vast domain. Settlers first met the Cherokees along the Appomattox River in Virginia, and slowly pushed them Southward to the lands of the Holston, Little Tennessee and Tennessee Rivers, an even into South Carolina. Before then, it is said, they made their homes in what was later to become the Eastern States.

The Cherokee usually painted or stained their olive skin with indelible ink. The men were large and robust; the women were tall, slender, erect, and had features of perfect symmetry.

History records that the Cherokee loved to dance, spending practically every night in this amusement. They excelled all other Indians, it is said, in this entertainment.

The Cherokees had no laws against adultery, and according to the British Lieutenant Henry Timberlake, they carried debauchery to greater excess than any other Indians except the Choctaws.
They were an extremely proud people, even to the extent of despising the lower class of whites. Although gentle and amiable to those they liked or knew as friends, once they took to the warpath, total destruction became their war cry.

The Cherokees had a simple procedure for the burial of their dead. When they determined that death was approaching, a grave was dug, and the body, even before death occurred, was prepared for its burial.

The Cherokees, as well as the Creeks, built their towns around a center square. This square was made up of four public buildings. These wooden structures, supported on posts that were stationed in the ground, faced each other.

The house of the chiefs faced the east and served those of the highest rank. The high chief, known as the Micco, used the center of this main building. On his right were the assistant Miccos, who were next in rank. They served as advisors in war. The second in order of rank were the advisors in civil affairs. They were housed in the area to the left of the Micco.

The warriors' cabin faced South on the square. The chief seat in this cabin was reserved for the head warrior. The others were seated to his right and left according to rank.

The cabin of the beloved men faced North. This cabin served the Micco's family as well as the families of other leaders of various ranks. The cabin of the young people faced the west.

Many early towns in the South adopted this pattern in laying out their business and government districts. This feature became known as "the town square."

At about 1700, there were 64 towns in the Cherokee Nation. However, due to wars with the French, English and neighboring tribes, this once great nation had been reduced to no more than 5,000 warriors by 1740.

THE CHICKASAWS

In general, the Tennessee River was the dividing line at the Muscle Shoals between neighboring Cherokee and Chickasaw tribes. At one time or another, there were some notable personalities in what was to become Colbert County - Chief Tuscumbia and Chief George Colbert, along with several of Colbert's brothers, who were also leaders in the Chickasaw nation.

In his later years, Chief George Colbert was granted a reservation across the river in West Lauderdale County. This area was referred to for many years as the "Reserve."

Unlike the Cherokee who came from the Northeast, the Chickasaws came from the west. They were fierce warriors who almost wiped out De Soto's expedition in Mississippi in 1541.

The warriors were described as raw-boned and slender, and inscribed their bodies with indelible ink. The females were slim, graceful, and almost always comely.

The Chickasaws had strict laws against adultery. The violators were severely punished by beating with poles and then cropping their ears. If caught the second time, the punishment called for cropping the nose or upper lip.

The family unit had two houses built, one beside the other. The summer house was an oblong-shaped cabin. Their winter house was of a circular form which was known as the "hot house." On cold nights they entered these tight small structures where fires were lit in the center of the room without the benefit of a chimney.

It has been said that history records no group of people on any continent at anytime who were cleaner than the Chickasaw. They practiced bathing every day, in summer and winter. Early settlers were amazed to see them break the ice at the riverbank so they could take their baths.

Some historians list their insistence upon cleanliness as one reason they sided with the English over the French and Spanish in the early Colonial wars.

The Chickasaws were great sportsmen, and were rarely beaten in their games. They often played ball for high stakes. Everybody, including the children, bet on the outcome.

The Chickasaw, as well as the Cherokee, became friends of the white settlers at the Muscle Shoals. However, they were finally forced to leave "the land of swift flowing and many waters in Alabama," for their new home in Oklahoma, beginning in 1837. The Cherokees had been removed earlier.

RELIGIOUS LIFE AMONG THE CHICKASAWS

The Chickasaws, who were encountered by the earliest white settlers at the Muscle Shoals, were a religious people. Hundreds of years prior to the arrival of the Christian missionaries they had developed a system of beliefs that governed their lives and social order, including the political affairs of their Nation.

They believed in a supreme being, "Ababinili," who was a composite force of the Sun, Clouds, Clear Sky, and "He that lives in the Clear Sky." The Sun was represented in each town by a sacred fire; coals from this fire were used to ignite the fires in every village home.

The Chickasaws had two Beloved Holy Men, called the "Hopaye," one chosen from each of the two great divisions of the tribe. Lesser priests assisted the Hopaye in performing their sacred duties. The medicine men, the "Aliktee," partic-ipated in the spiritual powers of the Holy Men.

Their spiritual world was filled with invisible spirits, witches, giants, and small people. The good spirits lived in the higher regions and, along with the small people, were responsible for bountiful hunts and other blessings. The small people also endowed the doctors with the arts of healing. The evil spirits dwelled among the darker shades of the West and, with the invisible giants, were blamed for bad luck and all personal and community disasters.

The Chickasaws believed in an existence after death, a judgment of the soul and a consignment to an eternal joy or an everlasting torment. Their burial rituals included essential steps in preparing for a journey that led to the judgment. The dead were buried in the floor of their homes in a sitting position facing the west. Weapons and other personal items were placed in their graves to accompany them on "their journey to the judgment."

Ceremonies played an important role in the religious life of the Chickasaw. The most important of these events was the Busk Festival, which was held every year at the beginning of the first new moon when the corn was ripe. The old sacred fires were extinguished and the ashes removed, at which time the new sacred fires were lighted.

Following rites of purification, the people feasted on roasting ears and celebrated with dance and music. This ceremony could compare in some ways to the American Thanksgiving and New Year's Day celebrations.

The Chickasaw people saw the physical universe in a spiritual context. They looked upon the changing of seasons, the animals and plants around them, and all other natural things as a part of their spiritual surroundings. Their religion colored tribal recreation and entertainment. Their music and dances served as spiritual as well as social functions.

The "old ways" of the Chickasaw people began to change with the arrival of Christian missionaries in the early 19th century. It was the missionary presence that finally stirred the Chickasaws to establish local schools. An 1830 report on the Caney Creek Mission School, which served Alabama and Tennessee, revealed, "the object is to give them (the Chickasaw students) acquaintance with the English language and the habits of civilized life."

KOGER ISLAND

Chealty, whose name was pronounced as "Che-aul-ty," was born on Koger Island in the Tennessee River about 1811 or 1813. She was never really sure as to what year. Her parents were Chickasaw people who lived in this Alabama section of the Chickasaw Nation. After the coming of the white settlers, her parents were baptized into the Christian faith at which time they adopted the surname, Smith, and Chealty became Charlotte Smith. At the age of 17 or 19 she was married to Josiah Higgins, reared a large family at Waterloo, and told interesting stories about her Chickasaw people as long as she lived.

Koger Island is one of a few islands below Florence that was not completely inundated when Pickwick Lake was formed in 1938. Prior to 1938, this island was separated from the North bank of the river by only a small-segmented stream of the river's flow. One could easily wade across to Koger Island except during times of high water.

In fact, Columbus "Pad" Smith, one of West Lauderdale County's most prosperous planters and merchants during the latter part of the 19th century, utilized Koger Island as part of his cotton-shipping operations. His wharf was extended across to Koger Island where boats were loaded for shipment to the large cotton markets.

Koger Island and Seven Mile Island are thought to have been either the center, or perhaps, the seat of government of a highly advanced group of pre-historic peoples more than a 1,000 years ago. They are referred to by archaeologists and anthropologists as the "Koger Island People." Their villages were located along the creeks and streams and on most all of the islands in this section of the Tennessee Valley. There is evidence that they used the large Florence Mound as a place of worship as well as for other ceremonies and rituals.

In the 1960's and 1970's, a display in the anthropology section of the Smithsonian Institute in Washington, D. C. referred to an abnormal practice of early Native American cranial deformation as those of the Koger Island People along the Tennessee River in Alabama. In a paper, "Red, White, and Black," published by Dr. Charles M. Hudson, in the 1971 issue of <u>Southern Anthropological Society</u> (University of Georgia Press) there is a reference to the "deformed round heads on Koger Island."

In his study, Dr. Hudson points out that this round head deformation differs from the under formed "long heads" of the "Shell Mound People," who had earlier lived at the Shoals. Both the Shell Mound People and the Koger Island People reshaped the heads of their infants by binding their heads to cradle boards in such a way that they were perfectly immobile.

Koger Island gets its name from the ante-bellum planter, William Koger, who purchased its 150 fertile acres as part of his plantation in the Reserve. Newton F. Neal originally purchased it from the Federal Government in 1820.

Koger Island and its neighbor, Seven Mile Island, are relics of an earlier millennium. They are as priceless archives of the 21st century that conceal an unspoken history of a highly advanced people who once lived along the Tennessee River at the Muscle Shoals.

THE LORE OF THE INDIAN LANGUAGE

The names of our state and the river which flows through our Muscle Shoals are monuments to the tongues of earlier peoples who once called this their home. The word "Alabama" is Muskogean and the name "Tennessee" is derived from the Cherokee.

The ancients in the Southeast spoke many languages, a number which were closely related. Quite a few, however, are now extinct. Yet, as reflected in some of our towns, creeks, rivers, and the designations of "Alabama" and "Tennessee," lives a haunting beauty of words that will never die.

The Chickasaw and Cherokee are generally the languages reflected by place names at the Muscle Shoals. The Chickasaw is of the Muskogean family, which includes five related groups: Chickasaw - Choctaw, Alabama-Koasati, Mikasauk-Hitchiti, Apalachee, and the Muskogee-Seminole.The Cherokee language is of the Iroquoian group which in ancient times was closely kin to the speech of thousands of Native Americans.

The Cherokee once knew the Tennessee River as "Kallumchee. " It is said that the Muscle Shoals was known as "Chaka tsh locko, "(meaning "big shoal") by the Cherokee, and as "Dagunahi, "(a place of mussels) by the Chickasaw. The Great Bend in the river from Huntsville to Waterloo was sometimes referred to as "Thegalego" by the Chickasaw people. Elk River is designated on early maps as "Chuwalee".

Old legends tell us that the Florence Indian Mound was known as "Wawmanona." Stories handed down by the original owners of the Sweetwater Plantation east of Florence say that it was named for the Cherokee "Succotania," which describes the bountiful sweet waters that flow from its large limestone spring at the head of Sweetwater Creek.

Old timers insisted that Shoal Creek was a singular word derived from the Cherokee "Ustanali, which meant "a place of rocks across a stream." Had it been plural, the Indian name perhaps would have been pronounced as "Chustanatuy" meaning "places of rock across a stream".

Probably the most picturesque of all place names was the Creek word "Tee kee ta no eh" for Lauderdale County's scenic Cypress Creek which winds and divides before it crosses the Tennessee line into Wayne County.

Chief Tuscumbia, or "Tashka Ambi" and his wife, "Im Mi Ah Key" were living near present Tuscumbia when the first white settlers arrived.

Sometime after 1822 they returned to Tashka Ambi's old home on the Tuscumbia River near Corinth, Mississippi. There the old "rainmaker" died about 1834 and was buried under the couch inside his house.

A study of vocabularies is always fascinating, especially when it includes a phraseology belonging to an art and knowledge given to us by ancient peoples. Such is the beauty of Alabama and the lore of our Muscle Shoals.

4 GEORGE COLBERT AND HIS TENNESSEE RIVER FERRY

An artist's conjectural painting of Chief George Colbert based upon descriptions of his likeness in early documents. (Pastel 30 x 40 inches, by artist Dorothy Carter McDonald, loaned by the Florence Indian Mound Museum.)

GEORGE COLBERT AND HIS TENNESSEE RIVER FERRY

"I was so enraged that had I not been cumbered with baggage I believe I should have ventured to swim it."

These were the impatient words of the ornithologist, Alexander Wilson, as he recollected the trouble it took to cross the Tennessee River about the year 1810. Traveling the Natchez Trace was difficult, but crossing at Colbert 's Ferry was exasperating.

Wilson arrived on the North bank late in the day and whooped and shouted until after dark. He couldn't have known that George Colbert had a rule never to cross the river at night. The next morning, after an uneasy night on the swampy North bank, he continued his loud calls for the ferry boat. It wasn't until aro-und 11:00 A.M. that Colbert's servants showed up to ferry Wilson across to the South bank.

Lorenzo Dow, the Methodist circuit rider, tells in his journal about using the ferry on October 26, 1804. He paid one dollar for each member of his party. This was the regular fee for man and horse. A man without a horse was half that amount. Post riders crossed at a special half fare. Colbert once complained that most white people who used his ferry were "Kaintucks". Many of them, he said, were poor and could not pay, and he carried them across free of charge. Most of his customers, though, were Indians, and George Colbert was never known to charge a blood brother.

Colbert's Ferry was a strategic location on the Natchez Trace. It played an important role in attracting the attention of men who would later return to develop, promote and speculate. Even before investors like John Coffee, James Jackson and John McKinley envisioned the potential value of its resources; George Colbert was enjoying its prosperity.

George Colbert was half Chickasaw. These Native Americans made their first recorded contacts with Europeans in the lower Mississippi Valley in 1540. After having befriended De Soto on his journey across Alabama and Mississippi, the famous explorer tried to enslave 200 Chickasaw warriors to carry his baggage. This was such an insult that they almost annihilated the Spaniards by setting fire to their lodgings and destroying most of their livestock.

George Colbert was said to have been half Scot. According to legend, his father, James Logan Colbert, pronounced "Kahl-burt", left Scotland, in January 1736, during the Jacobite uprising and sought refuge among the Chickasaws. He eventually became an influential member of the tribe, proving to be a brave leader in their wars. During the American Revolution, James Logan Colbert was a source of trouble for the struggling American colonies and her allies along the Mississippi.

James Colbert married three Chickasaw women. Two of his wives were pure Chickasaws and the third was a half-breed. His first wife gave him a daughter, Mollie. He fathered five sons by his, second wife: William, George, Levi, Samuel and Joseph. James Colbert's third wife bore him another son, James, and another daughter, Betsy. His sons became legends among the Chickasaws. Their father had tried to live in the ways of the Indians. The sons attempted to copy the life of the white man.

George, Levi, and James lived at various times in Mississippi and Alabama. All the brothers seem to have had more than one wife; their daughters and granddaughters were of such outstanding beauty that they wove interesting chapters of romance along the Natchez Trace.

After the Revolutionary War the newly established American government began the policy of awarding medals and military ranks to the more influential Indian Chiefs in the South. This was designed to lure them away from any potential alliance with the Spaniards. The Colberts were recipients of a number of these military titles. George was referred to in various documents as "Major" and "Colonel". At the end of his life he was listed as "General Colbert" by one newspaper.

The Colbert brothers were patriots, and at least two of them served in the American Army as scouts, guides and leaders of Indian detachments. William was with General Andrew Jackson in his campaign against the Creeks in South Alabama. One source shows George Colbert participating in the American Revolution under Washington. His military record reveals that he fought under St. Clair in 1791, and under "Mad" Anthony Wayne in 1794. He led an expedition against the Creeks in March, 1814, and served as a Captain in the U. S. Army under General Andrew Jackson from November 1, 1814 to February 28, 1815.

Levi, known as "the Incorruptible", became the most famous of the Colberts. Itawamba Mingo, as Levi was called by the Indians, was living near his brother George's ferry in 1805. Later in 1812, he opened his own inn, known as a "stand", on the Natchez Trace at Buzzard Roost Creek near the Bear Creek ford in what would become Colbert County in Alabama. In 1817 he moved to the Monroe County, Mississippi area. This was after he deeded his Buzzard Roost Inn to a daughter. She had greatly pleased her father by marrying Kilpatrick Carter, an early white settler.

In the Spring of 1834, Chief Levi Colbert set out for Washington on urgent matters pertaining to the negotiations for removal of the Chickasaw Nation. This would eventually send them to Oklahoma.

Along the way he stopped at Buzzard Roost where he became sick and died. It is not known whether they returned his body to his home at Cotton Gin Port, Mississippi, or if they laid the old chief to rest in the red soil of a county that would one day bear his name.

James, the youngest of the Colbert brothers, became a leader of great affluence among his people. His properties included a 500-acre plantation worked by over 100 slaves. He used his wealth to help pay the expenses of 50 Chickasaw families when they were forced to move to the Oklahoma Territory in 1837.

George Colbert, the ferryman, was called "Tootemastubbe" by the Indians. Historians have credited him as being one of two or three who guided the destiny of the Chickasaw during a critical period of their history. He was born in 1744 near the Tennessee River in what would become North Mississippi. In most of the treaties with the white man George served as chief negotiator. History records that he was quite shrewd in this role. He served as Chief of the Chickasaws for about twelve years.

Various accounts describing Colbert's appearance and character present an interesting study of this leader among the Chickasaws. Cyrus Harris, Governor of the Chickasaw Nation after their removal, described him as "illiterate but had some influence and stood tolerably fair; talk common English." A Methodist preacher called him a "very shrewd, talented man and, withal, very wicked." Dr. Rush Nutt, a Natchez planter, said that he was the "greatest of the Chickasaws, displays genius and talent...but is an artful designing man." Colonel Return J. Meigs, Cherokee Indian Agent, described him as: "extremely mercenary, miscalculates his importance, and when not awed by the presence of the officers of the government takes upon himself great airs."

Presbyterian Missionary Joseph Bullen of New York worked with the Chickasaws about four years. His journal, although mostly about spiritual matters, reveals interesting dialogues with people, especially the Colberts. On June 29, 1799, he was at the home of James Gunn who lived among the Chickasaws. This location later became Gunntown, Mississippi, near Tupelo. While there, Bullen said that Chief Colbert arrived "in a decent dress." Their religious discussion presents another dimension of George Colbert: "He informed me how he and his brother Levi had laboured to further the pious and benevolent designs of the Society; that he, Levi, and a number of others, wish to learn good things: no get drunk, but work, make corn, cotton, cattle, hogs, etc.

James Simpson grew up across the river at Florence. As a boy of ten years, he was fascinated when George Colbert and other Indians came to town and bought supplies at his father's store. As an old man, Simpson wrote about these scenes of the past and gave an interesting description of George Colbert: "He was tall and slender and handsome with straight black hair that he wore long, which came well down to his shoulders. His features were that of an Indian but his skin was lighter than that of his tribe. He wore the dress of a white man of his day and always appeared neat and clean. He frequently ate dinner at my father's house in Florence (Alabama). The building now known as the Commercial Hotel was my father's store and he had a reputation among the Indians as being an honest and just man and as a consequence of the Indian trade. Colbert often crossed the river in canoes with thirty or fifty of his tribe to purchase goods in Florence. The Indians seemed to enjoy roaming over the store looking at everything. They wore buckskin clothes of their own making. Some of them wore feather head dress".

George Colbert, according to one traveling preacher, "indulged in more than one marital adventure simultaneously." This was an accepted practice among the Chickasaws, especially if there were a number of unmarried sisters. He was a double son-in-law of Doublehead, the Cherokee chief who lived near Colbert's home. There is a spring at the site of his early home known as Doublehead Spring. Later, Doublehead founded a town near Brown's Ferry and one across the river at the mouth of Blue Water Creek in what was to become Lauderdale County.

Tuski-a-hoo-to, Colbert's principal wife, reputed to be the, fairest of all the Indian princesses, presided over Colbert's household at the ferry. Old families of Colbert County recalled with some amusement this rich Indian lady's refusal to ride in the elegant carriage provided according to her means. She followed this vehicle, which was driven by a slave, astride her favorite pony seated on a colorful blanket, and quite often she was barefoot.

Washington socialites were likewise amused when she accompanied her husband to a dinner at the White House dressed in the latest fashion and barefoot. It was a dark day for the Chief when Tuski-a-hoo-to died. He was never the same afterward. He buried her, according to a description in the 1834 Treaty, within sixty yards South of his dwelling house.

Colbert's other wife, Salechie, sometimes referred to as Shullechie, operated an inn on the Natchez Trace near Tupelo. One traveler, Edwin C. Thomas, wrote: "In 1836, I attended the land sales at Pontotoc. The first night in the nation I stayed at Salechie Colbert's, four miles west of where Tupelo now stands. She was a woman well fixed up, had a good house, and served a good fare."

These accommodations were quite different than those experienced in 1799 by the Presbyterian Missionary, Joseph Bullen:

> "**May 20, 1799**. We came to Big Town, weary, hungry, and myself unwell. Here we got hominy with milk, and bad water. The Indians appear to be poor but kind. With these I held some talk by the help of a Negro who could interpret. Lodged in a warm house on a bear skin.

> **May 21, 1799**. Could get nothing for breakfast, unless it were thin dried and damaged meat. This town consists of two hundred houses; is situated on a eminence, has good air, and an agreeable prospect, but is badly watered; they are a people generally less in size and stature than the whites. Most of them appear to have the manners of ancient simplicity; labour is done by the women, hunting by the men: Their visage differs but little from that of other Indians; their houses are made of poles, from three to five inches diameter, and plastered with mortar, are 16 feet by 22 on the ground, floored with earth, and covered with clapboards (sic)..."

Salechie outlived her sister, Tuski-a-hoo-to, who died prior to 1818, and accompanied her husband to the Oklahoma Territory in 1838. Salechie died February 1, 1846.

George Colbert had six children: John, Vicy, Susan, George, Jr., Vina, and Jane, and then Pitman Colbert who was an adopted son.

In 1801 the United States secured from the Indians the right to open a road through their land, "provided that the necessary ferries over the streams crossed by said road be the property of the Chickasaw Nation." This became the Natchez Trace. It followed a trail used by the Indians that had been in earlier times a buffalo run. Originally it crossed the Tennessee River at the mouth of Bear Creek. This was the location of George Colbert's first ferry, established about 1798. It was near, if not part of the site where his father, James Logan Colbert, once lived. Phillip Buckner, a Virginian, described his crossing at this place:

> "Got to Colburts (sic) at the ferry about 8 O'clock: got, 7 quarts of whiskey at 1 Doll per quart & 4 dried fish at 7 pce apiece: Cross't the River. J. Owing swaim the River J. Green broke one of the bottles of whiskey: went 3 or 4 miles; Dined; Sam'ls horse broke another bottle of whiskey; we then determined to drink the balance to save it; went on about 10 miles to a good run of water; Bell lost his coat behind him".

General James Wilkinson, the Army Chief of Staff under President Washington, sought George Colbert's assistance in laying out the route for the Natchez Trace. At Colbert's suggestion the crossing of the Tennessee River was relocated upstream to where the Twentieth Century Natchez Trace Parkway crosses the river at the General John Coffee Bridge. Wilkinson's report addressed this change:

> "I find, on inquiry and from observation, that the route by Bear Creek is an improper one, as the bottoms on both sides of the Tennessee are inundated for a considerable distance during the floods, and the ground over which it passes is hilly and much broken. I am, at the same time, informed by Major Colbert that a good way, and a good

crossing, may be found a little further to the eastward, which will shorten the distance."

The General was rather generous to Colbert. He agreed to furnish a new ferryboat to replace the one "worn out in the public service", as well as to build for Colbert the following structures: "Cabins for him, at such place as he may fix on, cabins for his own accommodations and that of travelers to include a kitchen and a small store house and stables, and be pleased to put up a strong pen. These buildings are not to cost more than the men's labor."

This became Colbert's Ferry and Inn on the South bank of the river. Although it was considered a good business in the wilderness, there were some years, especially 1806, when, according to Colbert, his income did not come up with expenses. Probably his most successful operations were for the U. S. Government. Congress was so astounded at his charges for ferrying Colonel John Doughty's Tennessee Volunteers across the river in 1803 that they sent Brigadier General James Robertson and Colonel Return J. Meigs to investigate.

Even after these charges were reduced, Congress delayed payment for another two years. It is not clear what the charges were for ferrying General John Coffee's command in 1813, but when General Andrew Jackson crossed with his troops in 1815, Chief Colbert submitted a bill to congress for $75,000. In all fairness, it is known that Colbert was disappointed with what the Army had built for him at the ferry site. The government, he said, did not live up to the promises made by General Wilkinson and his exorbitant charges were his means of recovering what he figured they rightfully owed him.

William Richardson of Boston, returning from New Orleans in 1815, arrived at the ferry while General Andrew Jackson's army was camped there. He wrote in his journal:

> "I however, being as wet as I could be, searched every building and at last found a place where I tied my horse without any permission from anyone. I left my friend to feed them and went to seek shelter for ourselves. In this I was, by way of bribing, very fortunate. I procured a little apartment for ourselves and retired from the noise of the soldiers from N. O. that filled every other part of the house."

Although the date of construction for George Colbert 's two-story house at the ferry was listed as 1808, some historians believe that the house was built earlier and was a part of the what General Wilkinson agreed to provide for the ferry. One historian, Frank King, of Leighton, Alabama, recorded the date as 1790. He inspected the old house in 1923 and wrote:

> "The house is built of the best heart material and fastened together with wooden pins. The two front rooms, one above the other, are twenty four feet by eighteen with a nine foot ceiling. The back room is the same size. The foundation is stone and the front porch is held up by well dressed black walnut columns, seven or eight inches square with the corners nicely beveled. The stone chimney, since the removal of the mantel, is the most attractive feature of the place. It is ten feet broad at the base, maintaining a width of eight for more than twenty feet from the ground where it tapers to about six. It was plastered with cement of a good quality. The mantel was sold to a Cincinnati party about 30 or 40 years ago for $100.00 and was stored in a Government building at

Riverton (old Chickasaw), which unfortunately was burned and the mantel lost."

In a private letter to Dr. James M. Glenn, Atmore, Alabama, dated April 26, 1928, King sent a photograph of the house along with the following note:

"You will notice the double stone chimney in this building is down but quite a lot of the old stones are yet to be seen. I remember years ago to have seen the chimney in good shape. I also remember a dozen or more Negro cabins which Colbert had for his Negro slaves. They consisted of four poplar logs about 30 inches wide to the walls of the cabins. They have long since fallen into decay."

One traveler, probably not having seen a decent dwelling during his long journey through the wilderness, was so captivated by Colbert's house that he described it as: "...a country palace with its abundance of glass in the doors and windows."

George Colbert was a spokesman for his people a number of years before he began operating the ferry on the Tennessee River. He continued in this role although his home was some distance from the center of the Nation located near what would become Tupelo, Mississippi. His first attendance at a conference with the white man was at Nashville in 1792. In 1794 he was among the Chickasaw delegates at Philadelphia, Pennsylvania. In 1801 he was involved in rather lengthy negotiations, and in 1802 visited Washington. His other services as Chickasaw spokesman were in 1805, 1816, 1818, 1826, 1827, 1830, 1832, 1833 and 1834. The last two meetings were in Washington D. C.

In 1806 Colbert sought the aid of the War Department in securing Cherokee recognition of the boundaries claimed by the Chickasaws. He didn't trust the Cherokee Agent, Colonel Return J. Meigs, even though Meigs was a friend of Colbert's father-in-law, Chief Doublehead. Colbert believed that Meigs was the source of the Chickasaws' troubles. He complained of white intrusion on Chickasaw lands in 1809, and threatened to drive them away himself. However, Colonel Meigs insisted that the intruders were on Cherokee and not Chickasaw lands. This was partially resolved when Meigs removed 201 squatters, although they were back in the area a year later.

George Colbert 's home at the ferry was the site of a significant conference between the Cherokees, Creeks, Choctaws, Chickasaws, and the U. S. Government in September 1816. His home was designated for this meeting as the "Chickasaw Council House."

Representing the government were Andrew Jackson, David Meriwether, and Jesse Franklin. At this conference the Chickasaws ceded their land North of the Tennessee River, as well as some territory south of the river. However, certain tracts were reserved. George Colbert was given sixteen square miles on the North bank of the river, including his ferry landing, in what eventually became Lauderdale County, Alabama.

He deeded this land back to the United States on May 15,1819. However, prior to this time he had sold certain parcels of land to white settlers, including a rather large farm to the Walston family that was located South of what was to become the Oakland community. Colbert's Lauderdale County land became known as "the Reserve." At one time a U.S. Post Office was located there with the designation as Reserve, Alabama.

According to one legend, Colbert and Jackson had an alter-cation during this 1816 Council when the General swung at Chief Colbert with his sword. A notch in one of the porch colu-mns was pointed out as where Jackson's sword hit when it mis-sed Colbert.

As with most old houses, Chief Colbert's home did not escape the inevitable ghost stories. As late as 1969 a former resident reminisced about her childhood days when her family lived in the house. She told about the eerie sounds that could be heard in the night, as if feet were ascending and descending the stairs. She reasoned, though, that it had something to do with the beams or rafters that were cut at angles which allowed the timbers to move back and forth as the temperature changed.

Frank R. King reported in the September 10, 1929 issue of *ARROW POINTS* the destruction of Chief Colbert 's home by fire. According to him, this happened, during the week of July 12, 1929.

On November 20, 1817, the U. S. Postmaster General, Return Jonathan Meigs, son of Colbert's old nemesis by the same name, issued a decree to the man responsible for the delivery of mail between Nashville and New Orleans: "Until further advised you can, agreeable to your letter of the 26th, pass the public Ferry on the Tennessee instead of Colbert's Ferry."

Two years later Meigs directed that the official mail route be charged so that it should follow the newly established Jackson's Military Road through Florence, and not the Natchez Trace. This ruling plus the opening of the Gaines Trace in 1817, in effect, cause the demise of Colbert's Ferry. Chief Colbert closed the ferry and inn that same year and moved to the Tupelo, Mississippi area.

History records show George Colbert played a major role in the treaties of 1832 and 1834 at Washington, D.C. In the latter treaty, a reservation consisting of four sections of land, was granted to Levi, George and Martin Colbert, along with Isaac Albertson and Henry and Benjamin Love. Martin Colbert was the oldest son of George's brother Levi Colbert.

This treaty also set aside a fractional section of land between the residence of George Colbert and the Tennessee River for George's own private use. This grant began at a point near Smith's ferry on the river and went South to Colbert's dwelling, and sixty yards beyond to include the burial site of Colbert's wife, Tuski-a-hoo-to. Also included in this grant was Colbert's Island.

After the Civil War the name "Georgetown" was generally in use as a description for what once had been called Colbert's Ferry. It is believed that Georgetown was named for Chief George Colbert. In the late 1870's Leander F. Hyatt operated a ferry at Georgetown. However, by 1872 he had abandoned it because of poor business.

George Colbert's plantation activities near Tupelo were typical of the emerging changes in the lifestyle of the Chickasaws. This came about partly through the influence of the white settlers. The influence of the Colbert family was quite significant as these changes began to occur, because of their great respect and admiration in the Chickasaw Nation. At the time of George Colbert's birth his people were living in a "Stone Age" culture. By the time of his death, they had abandoned the most characteristic features of a primitive society.

Benjamin Hawkins, General Superintendent of Indian Affairs in the South during this period, made this observation: "These people (the Chickasaws) are out from their old towns and fencing their farms. They have within two years fenced nearly 150, and all the farms have a Stock of cattle or hogs. The men begin to attend seriously to labor. Major George Colbert who ranks high in the government of his nation and was the speaker at the treaty with us has labored during the past summer at the plough and with the hoe. This example has stimulated others."

One of the great tragedies of American history was what is now known as the Trail of Tears, the hard and sorrowful removal of the Indians from their ancient lands. The Chickasaws were among the last to go. It was not until after Chief Levi Colbert's death in 1834, that negotiations finally went against them. There were no strong leaders to replace this man, and their removal was inevitable.

The first of the long lines to Oklahoma Territory from Alabama and Mississippi began in 1837. This has also been referred to as "the shadow of Jackson." No single individual was ever trusted and admired more by a people than Andrew Jackson was by the Chickasaws. Yet, it was Jackson who, more than any other man pushed for their removal from their ancestral home.

Colonel A. M. Upshaw of Pulaski, Tennessee, was placed in charge. He organized four migration centers in the Indian Nation: three in Mississippi and one in Northwest Alabama. The Indians were forced at bayonet point to leave their homes and enter these stockades, which were in effect, concentration camps.

Their main route was by land to Memphis and, then, by boats to the Arkansas River. Initially, 300 Chickasaws and Choctaws were placed on board a steamboat at Waterloo, Alabama on

July 13, 1837, and transported to Memphis. From there they were herded into boats destined for the Oklahoma Territory. Chief George Colbert and his family left aboard the steamboat Fox for their new home in the West on November 14, 1837 and they arrived seven days later.

Before leaving for his new home along the Red River, George Colbert presented his colorful sash and cap used during times of ceremony to a neighbor as a token of the friendship they had enjoyed. The sash was later donated by a descendant of this neighbor to the Indian Mound Museum at Florence. She presented Chief Colbert's cap to the Helen Keller Library at Tuscumbia. Chief Colbert also left behind a silver medal that had been presented to him by the President of the United States in 1801. Colbert gave this medal to Lewis Alsobrook whose family had settled in a small valley near the Alsoboro community in West Colbert County. Alsobrook, an employee of Chief Colbert, had been engaged to marry one of the old Chief's beautiful daughters. It was said that she broke the engagement because she did not want to be left behind when her family was removed to the Oklahoma Territory.

Although the Chickasaws endured better than the Cherokees, it was not uncommon for the long trains of horses and wagons to stop and bury their dead as often as four or five times in a single day. Their worst treatment was at the hands of white contractors who fed them spoiled meat and other deteriorated rations. When the Chickasaws reached Oklahoma Territory they were scattered into five relocation camps, some over one hundred miles apart. This, according to Colonel Upshaw, was due to the threat of smallpox among the Arkansas and Canadian River settlements.

The once brave Chickasaws who were feared by all other Indians, were afraid to occupy their western lands. They obtained permission from their old enemies, the Choctaws, to use part of their holdings until the Federal Government could send troops to protect them from the Kickapoos and other wild western tribes. They eventually moved to their own lands.

However, only about three-fourths of the tribe actually occupied the territory that had been set aside for them. Mingling with the Choctaws caused them to lose much of their identity as the once proud Chickasaws.

The Chickasaws received over three million dollars from surplus land sales they had vacated in Alabama and Mississippi. This amount provided annual interest payments of from $60,000 to $70,000, an average annual income of from $75 to $100 for each family. As a result these once proud people became idle, with some of the braves living in tents for the remainder of their days. Recognizing what was happening their agent, Colonel Upshaw, led them into a partial Renaissance that resulted in the Chickasaws becoming productive farmers in the Red River Valley of Oklahoma.

The Colbert's, along with the other wealthy mixed bloods, came to the western lands early in the removal period. They selected choice locations on the open tracts along the Red River, putting their slaves to work planting cotton and corn. They regularly returned to Mississippi and Alabama to look after their gins, mercantile operations and homesteads until they finally were forced to cut all ties, and to permanently relocate in their western lands. Chief George Colbert settled near Doaksville in the fall of 1838 after returning for a time to his former lands in Mississippi.

No individual worked harder than George Colbert to prevent his people from being uprooted and sent to the Oklahoma Territory. One of his final efforts was made on the streets of Tuscumbia where he gave a passionate speech on the behalf of the Chickasaw Nation.

In the Red River Valley near Durant and Ardmore, Oklahoma, almost at the Texas border, is the town of Colbert. There was a ferry at this place prior to the Civil War, and it, too, was known as "Colbert's Ferry". An elderly gentleman of this town, while reflecting upon his ancestors on a summer day in 1982, commented: "My father's talked of the hills and valleys and the land of swift flowing and many waters in Alabama. It was a good land. My people are poor in this country. My fathers lived good lives in Alabama."

Within two years after his removal from his ancestral home, Chief George Colbert was dead. An army officer stationed at Fort Towson, Arkansas, wrote about the event in a letter:

> **November 7,1840:** "We this day buried with honors of war, General George Colbert, the head of the Chickasaw Nation, a man of superior intelligence, the greatest of warriors, and the white men's friend... He was physically and mentally a great man; although (about) 86 years of age he walked as upright as a man of 25."

A Memphis, Tennessee, newspaper carried this notice:

> **Thursday, January 23, 1841:** "by a private letter, recently received from the far west, we learn that Colonel George Colbert, head chief of the Chickasaw Indians, died at his residence near Fort Towson, west of Arkansas, on the sixth day of November, aged 86 years."

The location of his unmarked grave has been lost in the passing of time. However, Colbert Park at the site of his old home on the Tennessee River, and Colbert County, Alabama, are the monuments to his life and influence at a place known as the Muscle Shoals.

THE FATHER OF THE COLBERTS

Colbert County is named for two Chickasaw brothers, George and Levi Colbert. George operated a ferry and an inn at the Tennessee River crossing of the Natchez Trace. About seven miles South of this site was another inn on the Trace operated from 1800 to 1817 by Levi Colbert.

The father of Levi and George was James Logan Colbert. It was once thought that James was born in Scotland. More recent evidence suggests, however, that he may have been born in North Carolina between 1722 and 1727. These sources indicate, too, that he was related to Joseph Calvert, who may have been his father or grandfather or perhaps a close relative. One family genealogist suspects that James' maternal grandfather was James Logan, a woodsman who traded with the Indians.

James Adair, an Indian trader, in writing about his experiences noted that James Colbert "has lived among the Chikkasah from his childhood." It is now believed that the young Colbert arrived in the Chickasaw Nation between 1736 and 1741, perhaps in the company of Abraham Colson, who made frequent trips among the Native Americans. Colbert eventually settled near what is now Bissell, Mississippi, and was married to three Chickasaw women; two were of full-blood and the third was of half-blood. There were eight known children by his three wives. His sons became legends among the Chickasaw. Although the father tried to live in the ways of the Indians, his sons attempted to copy the life style of the white man.

By the time of the American Revolution, Colbert had become a leader among the Chickasaw Nation who had sided with the British. In 1780 he led his warriors against Fort Jefferson which had been erected by the State of Virginia in what they believed was on Cherokee land. Afterwards he represented the Chickasaw in peace negotiations with Virginia. Later, one of these negotiators gave this description of Colbert: "From his education and mode of life, being bred among the Indians from his infancy, it will naturally be supposed he is illiterate, which is the case, but possessed of strong natural parts."

Colbert was involved in a number of campaigns against the Spanish who had entered the war on the side of the Americans in 1779. In May. 1782, he captured a boat on the Mississippi River which included among its passengers Dona Anicanora Ramos Cruzat and her four children. She was the wife of Lieutenant Colonel Francisco Cruzat, the newly-appointed Spanish Governor of St. Louis.

They were released after nineteen days of captivity upon promise to pay 400 pesos for the boat. In her journals, Madam Cruzat made some interesting observations about this dashing and handsome leader of the pirates, referring to him as a perfect gentleman.

In the spring of 1783, he led more than 100 warriors and Englishmen in an attack on Arkansas Post, a Spanish garrison. The post commander counter-attacked and Colbert was forced to retreat to his boats on the Arkansas River. This was not only

Colbert's last fight, it might have been the last skirmish of the American Revolution within the present boundaries of the United States.

Chief George Colbert 's home at the ferry on the Natchez Trace at the Tennessee River.

James Logan Colbert died almost a year later on a trip to the East Florida capital to report to his superiors. Some say he was thrown from his horse. Others speculate he may have been murdered by Caesar, his Negro slave.

Natchez Trace Key to Early Settlements

The earliest Chickasaw Path, which later became known as the Natchez Trace, crossed the Tennessee River at the mouth of Beech Creek about two miles west of Waterloo. Following a passage along high ridges, it entered Alabama some seven or eight miles North of Waterloo and crossed the river west of Beech Creek.

Today's Pea Ridge Road, North of Waterloo, generally follows this early path, although it originally led to the river at the mouth of Beech Creek Chief

The mantel at the residence of Chief Colbert in Colbert County, Alabama (photograph made about 1890 by Frank R. King, Leighton, Alabama).

MANTEL FROM RESIDENCE OF COLBERT, CHIEF OF THE CHICKASAWS. ERECTED IN 1790: ON SOUTH BANK OF TENNESSEE RIVER IN COLBERT RESERVE (NOW COLBERT X LAUDERDALE COUNTY, ALA:

George Colbert's first ferry crossed the Tennessee River here. Travelers on the early Trace were ferried across the river to the west side of Bear Creek a Chickasaw village was a short distance from this ferry landing, on the South bank of the river.

James Logan Colbert, Indian trader, is said to have lived in or near this village with one or more of his three Chickasaw wives; some historians think his son George was born here.

Among the early Natchez Trace travelers who crossed the river here were Kentucky, boat men, outlaws and pioneer preachers.

Colbert's original ferry site was the scene of an earlier Indian attack. An army officer, Major John Doughty, had been sent here in 1789 by President George Washington with a message to the Indians living in the old Southwestern Territory.

Waterloo, Alabama (about 1900). The original Natchez Trace crossed the Tennessee River a mile or two west of this site.

Reaching the mouth of the Tennessee River on Feb. 28, 1790, he proceeded with his party of 15 soldiers up the river to the mouth of Bear Creek, where he had planned a meeting with a delegation from the Chickasaw Nation.

However, Doughty was suddenly attacked by a party of Creek and Shawnee warriors who had at first seemed friendly. Doughty's report tells that five of his men were killed and six were wounded.

After 1801, Waterloo's original ferry site was moved several miles upstream to where the modern Natchez Trace Parkway crosses the Tennessee River.

The suggestion for this change was made by George Colbert to Gen. James Wilkinson, who was in charge of the army in the old Southwest.

In this capacity, Wilkinson had the responsibility of working with the Indians to establish and improve the Trace as a public road through their territory.

The location of the Trace through this corner of the state had a significant impact on the eventual settlement of the area. Those who crossed the river here went away to tell others about the beauty and bountiful resources of a place called the Muscle Shoals.

5 Chief Doublehead

The Wayside Inn was established by Daniel White as a stage coach stop from Huntsville to Florence about 1818. According to local legend it was the traditional home of Chief Doublehead and was built probably around 1800 according to the "ways of the white man." This log house was torn down in the 1960's to make way for the four-lane, U.S. Highway 72.

THE LORE OF CHIEF DOUBLEHEAD & HIS HOME

No man had a more profound impact on the early beginnings of what was to become Lauderdale County, in the Northwest corner of Alabama, than the Cherokee Chief Doublehead. He was to Lauderdale County what Chief George Colbert and his brothers were to Colbert County.

This strong, handsome, inflexible, and self-willed Indian would have made an interesting study in the modern science of psychology. He had a double personality that far outdid the fictional character that Robert Louis Stevenson assigned to *Dr. Jekyll and Mr. Hyde.*

Doublehead, or "Talo Tiske," meaning two heads, and sometimes "Autowwe," was a member of a prominent Cherokee family. One of his brothers was the beloved statesman, "Tassel" or "Old Tassel," a principal chief of the Cherokee Nation, whose name became in many ways a synonym for integrity and truth. One sister, Wurteh, married Nathan Gist, a white man who lived with the Cherokees and acted as an intermediate in their dealings with the whites. They became the parents of the most famous Cherokee of all, the notable Sequoya. Another of Doublehead's sisters married a Fort Loudoun soldier. Their offspring became the bold and magnanimous John Watts, who at one time was counted as the Chief of Chiefs among the Cherokees.

Yet, Doublehead was without influence or position until about the year 1790, when he established a town on the Tennessee River at the head of the Muscle Shoals. An early map of the Cherokee Country shows this village at a site near the South bank of Brown's Ferry below Athens. He later moved it to the North bank of the river near the mouth of Blue Water Creek, in Lauderdale County, Alabama.

There is evidence, supported by legend that Doublehead lived at other places in the Shoals area before settling at Blue Water Creek. Some sources say his home at one time was on the hill where James Jackson later built his Forks of Cypress, Northwest of Florence. Also, a map published in 1835 shows a Double Head Spring North of the town of Cherokee in present-day Colbert County.

Doublehead's position as a secondary chief plus the death of Old Tassel in 1788, launched his rise to a position of authority in the Cherokee Nation. From this time, until his death he became a power to be reckoned with, as he attended important conferences, usually as the head delegate, and exerted considerable influence in the negotiations of treaties between the U.S. Government and the Indian Nations. It was noted early in the reign of Little Turkey, who succeeded Old Tassel, that a local chieftain by the name of Doublehead was usurping much of the great chief's influence and authority, especially in dealings with the white government.

Doublehead's town site, near Center Star, was located where his brother-in-law, Tahleitoiskee, had lived before moving to Arkansas following the Treaty of Tellico in 1805. This location had the advantage of about a square mile of bottom lands that Tahleitoiskee's people had cleared and made ready for farming. These "Old Fields" at the mouth of Blue Water Creek were very fertile and appealed to the first white settlers, and subsequently, became the enticement that made this community the first to be settled in the county.

However, these rich bottom lands did not always produce an abundant. A drought in 1804, brought an appeal for help. The records of the Indian Agent at Hiwassee show some 300 bushels of corn were sent. Doublehead's people paid $110 for this relief, but this sum was later returned to the village by the War Department.

Inhabitants of Doublehead's town, originally about 40 in number, were mostly cast-offs from other Cherokee and Creek villages. This motley bunch became infamous in Tennessee history as "the ravagers of the Cumberlands." However, as the years passed, other and more respectable Indians, mostly Cherokees, moved in. And by the time of the arrival of the first whites, they were of the genial sort and, according to some diaries, made "mighty good neighbors."

This town site was in a disputed reserve that became known as the "Chickasaw Hunting Grounds." For over two hundred years both the Chickasaws and the Cherokees claimed these lands as their own. Thus, the settlement of the Muscle Shoals was cause for concern by the Federal Government, and especially General James Robertson, the protector of the Cumberlands.

However, the Cherokee Agent, Colonel Return Jonathan Meigs, thought Doublehead's settlement was an attempt by the Cherokees to test their title to that portion of the disputed Chickasaw Hunting Grounds. Robertson was finally calmed by the assurance from Chickasaw Chief George Colbert, who operated a ferry across the Tennessee at the nearby Natchez Trace that Doublehead was at the Muscle Shoals by his permission.

George Colbert was a double son-in-law of Doublehead. This did not go unnoticed by the diarists who traveled the Natchez Trace, especially by the circuit riding preachers. Tuski-a-hoo-to was the principal wife of the two sisters, and made her home with her husband at the ferry. Colbert's other wife, Salechie, operated an inn on the Natchez Trace near what would become Tupelo, Mississippi. Once again, Salechie outlived her sister, Tuski-a.-hoo-to, and moved with her husband to the Oklahoma Territory in 1837.

It's a popularly held belief that some of Lauderdale County's more prominent citizens are descents of Doublehead. There are other suggestions that Doublehead had several sons and that one, in fact, bore his name. This possibly could account for some confusion in the early records that show Doublehead's name on documents which were prepared several years after his death in 1807.

Old Tassel, head chief of the Cherokees, was a well-known friend of the whites. In the year 1788, he was invited, along with his son and two others, to the headquarters of Mayor James Hubbert under a flag of truce. Hubbert quartered the unarmed Cherokee party in a vacant house. Here, while he guarded the door, a youth who it seems had recently lost his parents to a party of Cherokee raiders, demanded revenge, and was handed a tomahawk by Hubbert, who even set up the scenario for the blood bath. Doublehead, upon hearing this tragic report of his brother's death, sought and found revenge against the white man.

He went on the warpath, and took his Muscle Shoal's Warriors with him. The very name of Doublehead and his raiding party brought fear and trembling to the white settlements between the Muscle Shoals and Nashville, and especially in the Cumberland Mountain area between Nashville and Knoxville.

Doublehead's first "hunting party" of record was in the fall of 1791. He had with him a group of 28 men plus women and children. Together they made a horrendous "scalping excursion" up the Cumberland. General Robertson sent an expedition to "get Double-head" on January 17,1792. This noble crusade, however, resulted in the death of five of Tennessee's finest men. Doublehead killed the three sons of Colonel Valentine Sevier, the noted brother of General John Sevier, and two of their friends.

The murder of Captain William Overall and a man named Burnett in 1793, at Dripping Springs, was gruesome and gory. Doublehead, it has been recorded, dishonored Overall's body by cutting away and eating the flesh from his bones, and dancing with his scalp in the Indian villages at Lookout Mountain, Willstown, and Turnip Mountain. In May of that same year, while meeting with a delegation of Chickasaws, he apparently alluded to this act of cannibalism when he said: "We, the Cherokees, had eaten a great quantity of the white men's flesh, but have had so much of it we are tired of it, and think: it too salty."

Doublehead was accompanied on many raids by his nephew, "Bench", and his brother, "Pumpkin Boy". Bench was a wild sort of fellow himself. Yet, on at least one occasion he tried to hold back his Uncle Doublehead in an unmerciful crime against women and children. Pumpkin Boy was a handsome warrior, well equipped with trinkets and a pair of silver mounted pistols. When Pumpkin Boy was killed by Sevier's men, his brother Doublehead, fierce and sullen by nature, proposed that every settler's cabin be burned.

Doublehead's state of mind over Pumpkin Boy's death led to what probably was the most unforgivable of all his crimes. This occurred at Cavet's Station in the fall of 1793. Doublehead was furious at his nephew Watts, who was head chief, for opposing his wishes to revenge his brother's death. Watts, it is said, almost revered his Uncle Doublehead and always treated him with utmost respect. However, this time he opposed the old warrior. Another important chief by the name of Vann sided with the head chief, Watts, and Doublehead, now in a fit of rage, took it out on Watts.

Watts had captured a little boy while assaulting a white settlement, and had the child on the horse behind him. Doublehead charged full force upon Watts and sank his flying tomahawk into the innocent child. Chief Watts managed to escape. Chief Vann witnessed this, and as long as he lived referred to Doublehead as "Kill Baby." Also, there are those who write that Doublehead was a wife beater; his wife supposedly died a horrible death.

The atrocities committed by Doublehead seem almost endless and unbelievable. Tennessee historian, Haywood, wrote that "he shed with his own hands as much human blood as any man of his age in America." It has been written that, "he was a stranger to all the softer and gentle passions. If he ever heard a love song in his nation he was unable to repeat it."

Some say that for a time Doublehead was "mad." Yet, this man, as bloody as his deeds were, was merely carrying out the ancient code of his people. The historian, Will Durant, wrote, in Volume 1 of *The Story of Civilization*, the first state in the evolution of law is personal revenge. "Vengeance is mine," says the primitive individual. Penology began with the "lax talionis" or law of equivalent retaliation. The Code of Hammurabi, two thousand years before the time of Christ, required that if a man knocked out an eye or a tooth, or broke a limb of a patrician; precisely the same must be done to him. Doublehead was honoring the most ancient of codes. He was doing to the white man what the white man had done to his brother Old Tassel.

The saga of Doublehead's warpath covers some six years; beginning in 1788, and ending, rather abruptly in June, 1794. Always ambitious, the eager chief had managed an appointment of importance and prestige. He became the leading delegate of a party of Cherokee chiefs visiting Philadelphia.

Here they met the first President of the United States, George Washington. It is said that Doublehead was the center of attention and was dressed in his most elaborate costume that was embroidered with a silver eagle design.

Later, following what must have been a long and drawn out negotiation with Secretary of War Henry Knox, Doublehead and the other chiefs in the party came away with their personal annuities increased from $1,500 to $5,000 annually. This enabled the crusty old warrior to go home and live in-style. Loaded with presents, he came back to Alabama by way of Charleston and reached Muscle Shoals, in October 1794. A lot had happened while the chiefs were in Philadelphia. On the way home he wrote Governor Blount a long letter concerning his meeting with the president. Two parts of this rather lengthy letter say something about the "new personality" of Chief Doublehead that emerges in history:

"**October 20th, 1794 Friend and Brother:** I send you this talk on my way home, just returned from my father the President. Now my brother, you know very well, and the rest of the white people, when I and some of my people went to Congress, we were sent by the head men of our country to go to that place. Now we have returned, and the head men and warriors, and the young men also are satisfied with what we have done, and are determined to hold the United States fast by the hand, and keep the peace. This is the talk of all, and I am glad to inform you, my friend, it is pleasing to me that I did not send my breath for nothing. It appears now we shall have a lasting peace now like brothers...We all mean to hold the talks given us by the President and General Knox, and we hope the white people will not let our hands go, but hold us by the hand as we mean to do them. I am, your friend and brother, Doublehead"

Determined now to copy the whites rather than to destroy their possessions and take their lives, he built what was then considered a pretentious story-and-a-half log house in the wilderness. This structure, which later, according to legend, became a stage coach inn, was nestled on the side of a hill that overlooked his village in the valley below. Here, according to early settlers, he lived at peace with man and became a well-known figure in various treaties between the Indian Nations and the Federal Government.

Emerging more and more as a spokesman for the Cherokee Nation he addressed the intrusion of their lands with the white man's roads. He spoke plainly his sentiments:

> "On behalf of my Nation I am authorized to speak to you. There are land speculators among you who say that we want to sell our land when we do not. ...there is a road that we have consented to be made, from the Clinch to Cumberland, and also the Kentucky Trace. When you first made these settlements, there were paths that answered for roads. These roads which you propose, we do not want made through our country. A great many people of all description will pass over them, and you would labor under the same difficulty that you do now. We hope that you will not make the roads through our country, but will use those you have made in your own limits. We hope you will say no more on this subject. I expect that you will think that we have a right to say yes, or no. I hope you will say no more about the roads, or about the lands. I am now done speaking for the day."

In the letter to the Indian Agent, written in 1802, he portrays the economic activities of life in his village at the Muscle Shoals, as well as in the Nation as a whole:

"Sir: When I saw you at the Green Corn Dance - you desired me to come & see you and get some goods from you - My intention is to come and trade with you. But I am so Engaged Hunting and Gathering my Beef Cattle that I expect it will be a moone or two before I can come - I... have now one Request to ask of you - that is to have me a boat Built - I want a good Keal Boat some 30 to 35 feet in length and 7 feet wide - I want her for the purpose of Descending the River to Orlians & back. I want her to be lite & well calculated to stem the Streem. I am Determined to by the Produce of this place & the Return by Water...I shall want two of your big guns to mount on the Boat - I am determined for to see up the White & Red Rivers in my Route & open a trade with the western wild Indians - Let me here from you soon –
I am Ser Your Reale Friend & Brother -
DOUBLEHEAD
Wrote by J. D. Chisholm who presents his Compliments."

The "white influence" that seems to have settled on Double-head's village, and even on the old chief himself, as evidenced by his writings, ties in with William Bartram's observation in 1789:

"… if adopting or imitating the manners and customs of the white people is to be termed civilization, perhaps the Cherokees have made the greatest advance."

Chief Doublehead's advisor and close friend was Captain John D. Chisholm, who lived among the Cherokees, and was a recognized member of the Cherokee Nation.

Suspicion has it that Chisholm became the major influence that led to Doublehead's other "personality" change as a friend and not a foe of the white settlers. After being associated with Chisholm, Doublehead began to walk as a gentleman, speak as a friend, and do business as if he had been educated at Harvard.

In 1802 he bought 100 barrels of flour for $2 a barrel from the operator of a boat that ran aground at the Muscle Shoals. He paid $20 and not a cent more and then when the owners offered to buy it back, he demanded no less than $8 a barrel. He was learning the white man's ways fast. He built a road from Franklin County, Tennessee, to the Shoals and tried to get the government to connect it with the main road to the Tombigbee settlements.

Doublehead had many good qualities. In a letter to a Knoxville newspaper shortly before Doublehead's death, he was described as brave and generous, with both white and red having experienced his liberality. His house was a haven for the needy, and on one occasion he wrote to the Indian agent asking aid for two poor middle-aged women living at his place with large families composed entirely of girls.

He was described as a friend to agriculture and domestic manufacturing. During the first half of 1801, thirty two pieces of cloth were woven in his town. Silas Dinsmore, agent to the Choctaws, passed through the Shoals in 1802 and met a white woman, a daughter of a Mr. Adams, then residing among the Cherokees. He described her as criminally lazy, mentioning the fact that although Doublehead had offered cotton, wheels, cards, and free board on condition that she and her sister would look after his house and keep it clean, neither of them had spun a single thing during his whole stay. Dinsmore was also shocked because these two sisters went about dressed in men's clothing.

During a meeting between Doublehead and other Cherokee leaders with Secretary of War Henry Dearborn, on January 7, 1806, a large tract of land was reserved for Chief Doublehead.

Upon the advice of John D. Chisholm, the Doublehead Company was soon formed by Doublehead, along with another Cherokee by the name of Checkout, and Chisholm, who also served as Doublehead's agent, power of attorney, and legal counselor. This Indian land development agency literally leased thousands of acres of land in the area between Elk River and Cypress Creek to more than fifty white settlers. Almost 200 years later descendants of the following people are still living at the Muscle Shoals: McConnell, Lucas, Porter, Phillips, Burney, Butler, Chisholm, Johnson, Hays, Moore, Riggs, and others.

Doublehead's Reserve, however, was not officially open for this type of settlement, and certainly not sanctioned by the Cherokee Nation. After Doublehead's death in the summer of 1807, troubles began for these lease holders. The Cherokee Agent Meigs had the intruders evicted in 1811.There is a petition showing that the movement to drive out the whites was under way as early as 1809. A document in the W.S. Hoole Special Collections at the University of Alabama Library reveals that these "first families" were still trying to recover at least part of their investment as late as 1827.

The end of Doublehead was a tale of horror. It was about as dreadful as the crimes Doublehead had committed against the whites in the Cumberland's. The man who recorded these events was none other than one of the most famed of all Indian fighters - General Sam Dale. This gory story begins with a great ball game in the Cherokee Nation on the Hiwassee River in the summer of 1807. During the festivities after the ball game Doublehead greeted the General, with whom he was well acquainted, with a bit of dry humor:

"Sam, you are a great liar. You have never kept your promise to come to see me." With a smile illuminating his grim features, he offered Sam Dale a drink from his bottle of whiskey. The bottle was emptied, and Dale, in return, offered Doublehead a drink. The old Indian replied: "When in white man's country, drink white man's whiskey, but here, you must drink with Doublehead."

Serious trouble began almost immediately afterwards when Doublehead was accosted by a fellow chief by the name of Bone Polisher. He denounced Doublehead as a traitor, referring to Doublehead's trip to Washington on January 7, 1806, with Chief Vann, Chief Taluntuskee and Colonel Return J. Meigs. At that time the Cherokee delegation ceded all the area between the Tennessee and Duck Rivers, except for Double-head's Reserve.

As matters quickly reached a boiling point, Bone Polisher drew his tomahawk and rushed upon Doublehead, but was shot through the heart by the wiry Doublehead. After killing his adversary, Doublehead made his way, wounded and bleeding, to McIntosh's Tavern. Here he encountered another old friend, John Rodgers, a white man and Indian trader. Major Ridge, a Cherokee, was also there. He would later become a soldier and hero under General John Coffee during the famous Battle of Horseshoe Bend, August 27, 1814, in South Alabama. Another character present at McIntosh's Tavern at the time was Alex Saunders, a half-breed. All three men were to play roles in the struggles that followed.

John Rodgers took up the quarrel that had cost Bone Polisher his life. Old man Rodgers had lived among the Cherokees since before the American Revolution. He had an honorable record, and was the ancestor of America's Twentieth Century humorist, Will Rogers. Doublehead proudly rebuked his old friend:

> "You live by sufferance among us. I have never seen you in council nor on the warpath. You have no place among the chiefs. Be silent and interfere with me no more."

But Rodgers was a stubborn man, or maybe he had lived among the Indians too long. He wouldn't back off, and Doublehead drew his pistol to fire. The fact that the wounded chief had been drinking, and had failed to reload his pistol after killing Bone Polisher, was probably why John Rodgers survived and went away to tell again and again of his narrow escape from the hands of the bloody Doublehead.

This episode with the trader, John Rodgers, gave the others time to act. Someone managed to extinguish the tavern light, and instantly a pistol shot rang out from a dark corner of the room. When the light was restored, Rodgers, Ridge and Saunders had fled and Doublehead lay motionless on the floor. The ball had shattered his lower jaw and lodged in the nape of his neck.

Friends pulled the mortally wounded chief from the building, and across a field, and hid him in the loft of the schoolmaster at Hiwassee. But they left a trail of blood, which was easily followed, by Major Ridge, Alex Saunders and two clansmen of Bone Polisher. When they arrived the dying warrior was lying on the attic floor in a pool of blood. Showing no mercy, not even to the dying, both Major Ridge and Alex Saunders drew their pistols with the intent to finish off their adversary. But the hand of fate that had been so busy that night again intervened, causing both pistols to misfire.

This seemed to be a clue in this dialogue of death, for old Doublehead suddenly sprang to life and physically attacked Major Ridge with almost super-human strength. Sam Dale wrote that Doublehead would have overpowered Ridge had Ridge's partner, Alex Saunders, not shot Doublehead again, this time through the hips and then jumped him with his tomahawk swinging.

Doublehead managed to wrench free, and leaped again upon Major Ridge. This gave Saunders time to grab another toma-hawk and drive it with full force into the skull of the dying Doublehead. As Doublehead fell to the floor again, one of Bone Polisher's tribesmen crushed the old warrior's head with a sharp spade.

At last, Doublehead was dead. He was no ordinary man, and this was no ordinary death. He died as he had lived, and it took a room full of enemies to bring him down. Ironically, Major Ridge, who played a key role in this execution, came by a similar fate some thirty years later in Oklahoma.

Historians have analyzed the killing of Doublehead to be evidence of a growing sense of unity on the part of the

Cherokees. Hemmed in by white settlements they were coming to the realization that no longer could each chief be a law unto himself if they were to survive as a Nation.

Doublehead's death was an embarrassment to Colonel Meigs, the Cherokee Agent at Hiwassee. It was later learned that these two were to have worked together in establishing the eastern line of the recent Cherokee cession in such a way as to include considerably more land than had been ceded.

Cotterill, the historian, states that Colonel Meigs drove the Cherokees out of the Blue Water Creek village following Doublehead's death, and he burned the home of the old chief.

The lore of Muscle Shoals is filled with its own version of stories. Legends have been passed from generation to generation. One legend tells that the friends of the old chief carefully brought his bones and back to Alabama. Based upon ancient Cherokee burial customs, his body would have been stripped of flesh and only his bones conveyed to his grave for burial.

Two graves have been pointed to as the possible sites of his resting place. One is at the top of the hill behind where his log house stood. The other grave is in the bottomland about where Doublehead's village once stood. Kit Butler, an ex-slave who met the stagecoaches and tended to the horses at the Wayside Inn, remembered the "awesomeness of that Indian's grave upon the hill above the house." Old Doublehead's spirit, he said, "would rant and rave on that hill, especially on dark and stormy nights."

Tall tales and whispers have persisted for almost 200 years in Lauderdale County about Double-head's cave and the hidden riches. The most common description defines a cave alongside the bank of the Tennessee River, marked by the carving of a turkey's foot in a nearby rock. One of the turkey's toes was supposed to have pointed the way to the hidden entrance. There was a cave alongside the old Muscle Shoals Canal, just west of the mouth of Blue Water Creek that was known as Doublehead's Cave. This cave was covered by the backwaters of Wheeler Dam in the early 1930's.

One legend is often repeated concerning the construction of Wilson Dam. This involves the appearance of an elderly Indian during the summer of 1925, just as the backwaters of the dam were beg-inning to rise. This stranger from the Cherokee Res-ervation in Oklahoma had sketches of the river from Shoal Creek to Elk River. He asked many questions, but the one rem-embered most was about the rock that had a carving of a turkey's foot.

Mollie Stutts recorded in her memoirs that early settlers around Green Hill in Lauderdale County pointed out a large cave on Possum Creek between Killen and Green Hill as the place where the silver was hidden. Old people in the western section of Lauderdale County pointed to a cave near the Central Heights community where a carving of an Indian with a double face once guarded the entrance that long ago caved in and can be seen no more. Even the old timers across Elk River in neigh-boring Limestone County knew of a cave where, according to legend, several barrels of gold and silver were stored.

Probably the most intriguing of all the stories about Double-head's cave can be found in the account as told by the early historian, Judge William Basil Wood of Florence:

> "It is a well known fact that Captain Chisholm, the grand-father of our respected townsman, T. L. Chisholm, Esq.,

visited this County, in the early part of the century. He was on very friendly terms with the Cherokees, and the Chief Double-Head. At the invitation of Double-Head, he visited the cave where the Indians were smeltering and working the silver ore. Before, however, he was permitted to enter the cave he was blindfolded, and his horse being led, was caused to travel many miles, by Indian paths and through the woods, so as to be bewildered, that he might not retain any idea of the route he came. After he entered the cave the bandage was removed from his eyes and he was permitted to see the work of extracting the precious metal from the ore going on. Double-Head presented him with several bars - not quite as large as a fence rail - which he carried with him to Tennessee."

Legends and history sometimes almost mingle as one, and the lot of the historian is hard as he attempts to decipher which is truth and what is fiction.

Judge Wood's memoirs also tell of an event, about 1840, when several men, including two prominent citizens, Levi Cassity and James Thompson, explored a cave some-where above Shoal Creek. They found working tools and crucibles, which they concluded were left by the Indians. They believed they had discovered the legendary cave, and came to Judge Wood, he recalled, in an attempt to purchase the property. The owner of the land refused to even discuss the proposal, much less sell the land. Levi Cassity died several years afterwards and James Thompson moved to Mississippi, leaving no directions to the location of the cave.

According to another old tale, two men named Borland and Coulter found a cave near the mouth of Second Creek which had been carefully closed with a stone. It contained an Indian ladder descending some 20 feet, and some-thing similar to a blacksmith's hearth, but no silver.

Legends and history sometimes almost mingle as one, and the lot of the historian is hard as he attempts to decipher which is truth and what is fiction. However, the name of Doublehead is entrenched among the hills and hollows in Lauderdale County, and forever engraved in the earliest archives of a people called the Cherokees.

Old Doublehead did indeed live a double life. His death was as extraordinary as was his dual personality. The colorful saga he left to the Muscle Shoals on the Tennessee River will never fade away as long as there remains one aged record or one old legend to whet the curiosity of future historians.

THE LEGEND OF OLD JOHN MELTON

They say that old John Melton came from Ireland and married a sister of Cherokee Chief Doublehead. It is known that he settled among the Cherokees and that he built a commodious log house on the South bank of the Tennessee River almost directly across from the mouth of Elk River. Here, for many years he operated an inn for travelers. One guest went so far as to say that he "never fared better in any part of the United States, but their bill was excessively high."

As early as 1770, the Lower Towns of the Cherokees had established Melton's Bluff as an outpost against the encroachment of the Shawnees and Chickasaws upon their hunting lands. The Cherokees soon began using it as a fortress at the Muscle Shoals to keep out land speculators and to block the passage of white emigrants who were attempting to navigate the Tennessee River as a route to the Natchez District in Florida. Luckless flatboats and keelboats often ran into trouble as they approached Elk River Shoals, at the upper end of the Muscle Shoals. The Cherokee warriors, who were watching from Melton's Bluff, would then attack, rob, and sometimes murder the passengers and crew.

Leaders of these Cherokee pirates have been identified by some historians as "The Glass," "Bowie," or some lesser known warrior. Others have insisted that the Irishman John Melton was the man most responsible for the boat raids, although this has never been proven. Anne Newport Royal, America's first female correspondent, visited Melton's Bluff twice in 1818. These were timely visits in that Melton had been dead only two or three years. Following her inquiries about John Melton, she wrote in her journal: "with the assistance of the Indians, he (Melton) used to rob the boats which passed down the river, and murder the crews. By these means he became immensely rich, owned a great number of slaves, most of whom he robbed from these boats."

John Melton and his Cherokee wife had a number of children; the names of some of them are believed to have been Moses, James, Charles, David, Thomas, and Merida. Following the 1806 treaty with the Cherokees, Moses Melton was made beneficiary of one of the tracts of land reserved by the provisions of what became known as the "Cotton Gin Treaty." James Melton was one of the noted, pilots who would "hire out" to the boats going down the river. After successfully guiding the boats over the hazardous Muscle Shoals, James would walk back to Melton's Bluff to wait for another river craft who needed his service. One of John Melton's daughters, probably

Merida, was married to another Muscle Shoals pilot named Rhea. Following the Creek Indian War, Charles Melton moved eastward on the Tennessee River and founded the Cherokee village called Meltonsville.

It has been written that Chief Doublehead's assassination in 1806 may have caused John Melton to fear for his own life.

According to Anne Royall's journals, the old man soon moved to a large farm on the North side of the Tennessee River where he built a fine house "and died rich and in a good old age."

MILITIA OVERTAKES INDIANS AT ELK RIVER

The backwaters of Wheeler Dam conceal a number of historical sites. One is an early battlefield where blood was shed between white settlers and the Cherokee Indians more than 200 years ago. A bloody skirmish between the Tennessee militia and Chief Doublehead's warriors occurred near the mouth of Elk River in 1793. At that time, Monietown, on the South bank of the Tennessee River, was the main Cherokee village at the Shoals.

However, Doublehead had established a camp near the mouth of Elk River in what is now Lauderdale County. This camp was connected to Monietown by a winding ford, which crossed over two small islands in the middle of the river and the larger Gilchrist Island alongside the South shore. Around 1800, Doublehead established his home and village near the mouth of Blue Water Creek between Center Star and Elgin.

The fight at Elk River followed one of Doublehead's terrorizing raids around Nashville in 1793. His warriors had killed and scalped a man named Helan who was clearing land for Jonathan Robertson, one of the early settlers in that area. An alarm was sounded, and a force of 110 militiamen, led by Captain Thomas Murray, was soon in pursuit of Doublehead and his warriors.

Captain Murray ambushed the Cherokees at the mouth of Elk River. Upon entering this stronghold, Murray discovered that seven of the enemy had been killed or drowned during his attack on the camp. During this brief pause in fighting, four warriors suddenly rushed into the front lines of the militia, two of whom were killed immediately.

Another warrior, described as a large and surly fighter, refused to run and was shot several times with rifle fire which failed to bring him down; he was then shot in the back with a musket loaded with buckshot. Following the battle, measurements were made of this fatal buckshot wound; a total of sixteen shots had entered the warrior's back within a circumference of six inches.

Two of Doublehead's men were found hiding under a nearby bluff. One, wounded in the arm by a militia sharpshooter, was later shot through the head as he tried desperately to conceal himself in a crevice under a bluff close to a nearby creek. The second Indian jumped into the river and attempted to swim away but was pierced by half a dozen shots from the bank. It was reported that four additional warriors were killed as they attempted to flee across the ford, but their bodies were too far out in the river to be retrieved. Captain Murray and his men took seven scalps back to their homes in Tennessee as trophies of the battle that was fought on the banks of Elk River in the territory that was to become Alabama.

This skirmish did not end Doublehead's terrorism against the white settlers in Tennessee. His horrendous "scalping excursions" began in 1788, and ended rather abruptly in June, 1794.

Although the Tennessee militia had made two earlier expeditions during 1787 to the Muscle Shoals to eradicate the presence of marauding parties of Creeks and Cherokees, this battle at Elk River was the only known campaign against Doublehead and his warriors to occur in Lauderdale County.

THE LURE AND LORE OF DOUBLEHEAD'S CAVE

For almost 200 years stories have been told about Doublehead's Cave at the Muscle Shoals. A number of these tales are about an underground cavern where Doublehead processed silver ore. This has been discounted by a number of geologists who say it is highly unlikely silver ore has ever existed in this area.

One account of Doublehead's silver processing can be found in Matthew Powers Blue's unpublished manuscript which was based upon material he had gathered during the 1850s. Chief Doublehead, according to Blue's history, allowed his friend John Chisholm to visit this cave. After reaching Doublehead's Bluff, located near the mouth of Blue Water Creek, Chisholm was blindfolded and placed on a horse. The Indians then led the horse and rider a distance of about three and a half hours, during which time they crossed over some small streams. Blue's description of the cave is as follows:

> "...he was taken into the cave and there found a large quantity of silver with some apparatus for melting it... When they came out, the bandage on his eyes was replaced but they had been less careful and by raising his head, he discovered that they started off west as the sun was but an hour or two high. They reached Doublehead's (home) in half the time it required to come."

Judge William Basil Wood gave a similar story of Chisholm's visit to Doublehead's Cave in an address he made at Florence on July 4, 1876. Chisholm returned to this area following Doublehead's assassination in 1806 but was unable to locate the cave.

Blue tells another story of the exploration of a cave near the mouth of Second Creek by two men named Bourland and Coulter. After removing a large stone which covered its entrance, they descended into the cave on an Indian ladder, which had been left there, to a depth of some twenty feet to the floor of the cavern. There was no evidence of silver, but did see what looked like that of a blacksmith's hearth.

About 1840, James Thompson, Levi Cassity, and others explored a cave somewhere above Shoal Creek and found tools and crucibles, which they concluded were left by the Indians. An attempt was made to purchase this site, but the owner refused to sell. Cassity died soon afterwards and Thompson moved to Mississippi; they left no directions as to where the cave was located.

One story was told by a worker at Wilson Dam. He remembered that just prior to the flooding of the land behind the dam, an elderly Indian showed up with a crude map of the area from Shoal Creek to Elk River. This stranger questioned the workers about whether they had seen a large rock near the river which, he said, had art engraving of a turkey's foot on it.

Even General John Coffee added to the mystery of these shores. In 1817, while surveying Melton's Bluff, across from Rogersville, he reported a magnetic attraction that caused an imperfection in his survey for a distance of about twelve or fifteen miles.

If there is a Doublehead Cave, then surely it lies hidden today under the peaceful waters of either Wilson or Wheeler Lake. This land between Killen and Rogersville has long held a certain lore associated with the early Indians.

SALT CAVE ON THE DOUBLEHEAD RESERVE

During the War of 1812, the Secretary of War granted to LeRoy Pope of Huntsville the authority to establish mining operations at the Saltpeter Cave on the Doublehead Reserve near Rogersville. Meanwhile, the Cherokee Nation gave similar rights to John Walker and John Lowery. On January 7, 1813, the Cherokee Agent at Hiwassee gave permission to all three men to work this cave as long as "the peace and quietness of the Indians be not disturbed."

The main entrance to Salt Cave is now covered by the back-waters of Wheeler Dam. A smaller opening was said to have been located some distance from the river.

Major W.R. King's 1885 Muscle Shoals Canal Map shows a range of high bluffs near the mouth of this underground cavern. On the opposite bank was a long and narrow stretch of marshlands known as "Tennessee Island."

Local folklore has been passed down over many generations about Salt Cave. There are stories about a man called "Crazy" who once lived under the shelter of the entrance to this underground chamber.

Good descriptions of Salt Cave can be found in the stories as told by Stanley Wesley Laird who grew up in Limestone County.

He recalled that the entrance to this chamber was about equal in height to a "two-or-three-story building." Laird described a number of labyrinths inside the cave that extended several miles back from the bluff. While exploring the cave, Laird and a boyhood friend found a petrified turtle near the cave's entrance. This unusual find was similar to the discovery of a petrified sea turtle in a large cave near Huntsville in 1820. It is believed the Huntsville sea turtle lived during some ancient eon known as the Paleozoic Period. Roughly, the Northern third of Alabama is said to have been covered by what geologists refer to as the shallow Cretaceous Sea.

Salt Cave was one of a number of local underground caverns thought to have been used by Chief Doublehead to hide his stolen silver, gold and other treasures. Legend has it, these precious metals were melted and molded into bars inside the cave. This local Cherokee staged numerous raids into middle and eastern Tennessee, beginning in 1788 and ending rather abruptly in June, 1794.

OTHER LOCATIONS OF "DOUBLEHEAD'S CAVE"

Another legendary "Doublehead Cave" was located several miles downstream at the mouth of Blue Water Creek near the Doublehead Bluffs. An early resident of East Lauderdale County believed Doublehead's Cave to have been located on Opossum Creek near Killen. One cavern near Central Heights had an Indian carving at its entrance showing two Indian heads. And Limestone County had its own version of "Doublehead's Cave." Another of these legendary treasure places was said to have been located near the mouth of Big Nance Creek on the South bank of the Tennessee River. According to an old newspaper clipping, a Major James Johnson visited this site prior to the Civil War at which time he discovered three skeletons, three Spanish battle axes, and several Spanish coins.

Dark underground caverns have been both a mystery and an intrigue since the dawn of time. It would be most unusual to find one in any corner of the world that did not have its own story. Those found among the limestone cliffs and hills at the Muscle Shoals have added color when linked with the legend of Chief Doublehead.

6 Chief Bigfoot and Chief Glass

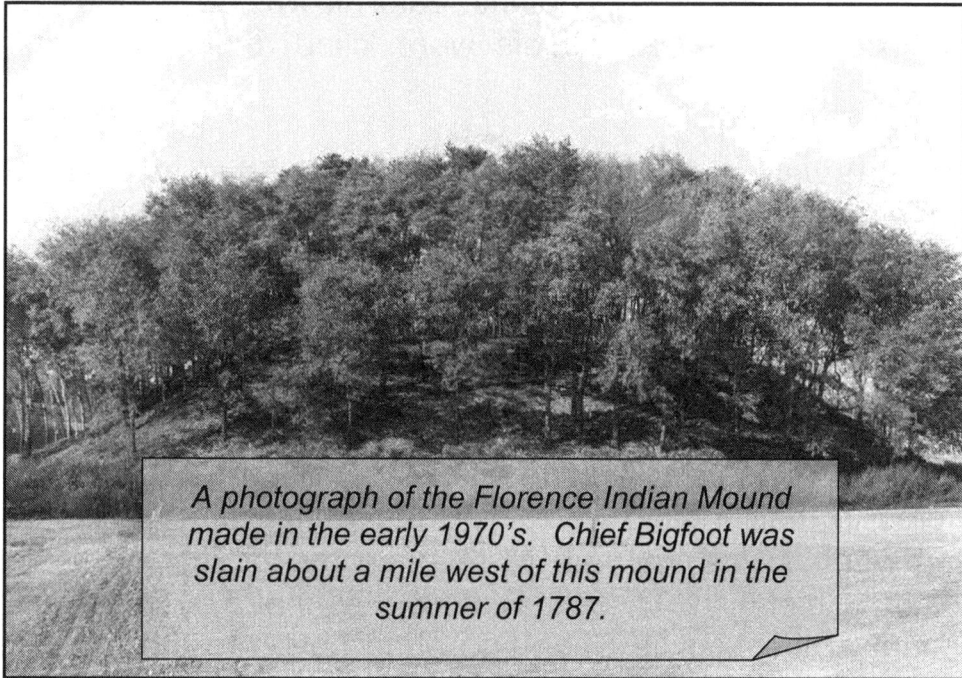

A photograph of the Florence Indian Mound made in the early 1970's. Chief Bigfoot was slain about a mile west of this mound in the summer of 1787.

CHIEF BIGFOOT SLAIN IN LAUDERDALE COUNTY

In the late 1780's, before the era of Chief Doublehead, no Indian was feared more by the white settlers on the Cumberland River than Bigfoot. Both Bigfoot and Doublehead used the sparsely populated Chake Tshlocko, which was translated into the English as "Mossel Cholls", and later as "Mussel Shoals", for their base of operations as they raided and plundered Middle and Eastern Tennessee.

Bigfoot and Doublehead had a number of similarities. Each in his own way made war against the white man. They were ruthless, bloodthirsty and deadly. Both were warriors and chiefs and, in some respects, employed the same tactics. After a surprise attack on a farm or community, they would hastily retreat back to their respective villages at the Muscle Shoals on the Tennessee River. The Tennessee was known as the Hogohegee River by the Indians. Later, it was called the Cherokee River. Also, both Chiefs were killed during their prime years.

But there were marked differences. Doublehead was a Cherokee and Bigfoot was of the Creek Nation, which was generally located in what later became Eastern Alabama. Although they were both chiefs, Doublehead was of regal lineage and claimed his title by right of birth. His family had ruled the Cherokees for generations. Bigfoot's title was self-made by his own power and was of no consequence in the Creek Nation. He was chief only in his own village and among his small group of warriors. They differed in their motive for raiding the white settlers. Doublehead went on the warpath to revenge the death of his older brother, Chief Old Tassell. Bigfoot was paid by the French Traders at the Muscle Shoals to bring havoc to the American settlers around Nashville.

Although they both were killed, Doublehead died at the hands of his own tribesmen. Bigfoot was killed in battle at the hands of a Tennessee Volunteer. But the most significant difference was, although they were enemies of the white settlers, Doublehead lived to make peace with the Americans and became a friend of the first whites to settle at the Muscle Shoals.

It is not known whether Doublehead and Bigfoot knew each other. Some historians believe that Doublehead was connected with the village at Tuscumbia known as Oka Kapassa, or Cold Water, and there is some suspicion that he led their earliest raids into the Cumberland Valley. No existing document, however, connects Doublehead with raids into Tennessee prior to 1791.

However, it is almost certain that Chief George Colbert of the Chickasaw Nation was not personally acquainted with Bigfoot. Colbert was born in 1744 on the banks of the Tennessee near what is now Iuka, Mississippi. It wasn't until probably 1798 that he began his ferry operation in what is now Colbert County, Alabama. For some reason the Chickasaw Nation was not aware of the existence of Oka Kapassa. According to what evidence is available, it was accidentally discovered by two Chickasaw warriors. It was the Chickasaws who informed Colonel James Robertson at Nashville of its location at the Muscle Shoals.

After the murder of his brother, Colonel Robertson led an expedition to the Muscle Shoals in June 1787. With 130 men and two Chickasaw guides he proceeded down the Doublehead Trace, which ran from Duck River to the mouth of Blue Water Creek. His report reads that upon hearing the roar of the waters at the Muscle Shoals he halted his men about ten miles from the river from where he dispatched one of his Chickasaw guides and several of his soldiers to the mouth of Blue Water Creek. Upon returning about midnight they reported the distance was too far to reach before dawn. The following day Robertson made his way to the high ground above the river at the site that would in 1818 become the town of Florence.

It was at the future site of Florence that Colonel Robertson discovered a well traveled Indian road that ran from the mouth of Cypress Creek to the mouth of Blue Water Creek. It followed the high ridges, entering the future town of Florence from the North along what is now Hermitage Drive. It turned east at about where St. Bartholomew's Episcopal Church is located on Darby Drive, and through the Hickory Hills Subdivision where it crossed close to the Lauderdale County Board of Education

Office on Middle Road, and then along the same route as followed today by U.S. Highway 72, to Blue Water Creek.

Photograph of Chief George Colbert's home made before it burned in 1929. The dog-trot style log house at the rear of the main house was used as a barrack for lodging travelers on the Natchez Trace later; it was used for slave quarters. Chiefs Colbert and Tuscumbia were contemporary residents of present day Colbert County, Alabama.

After dispatching a small scouting party on this Indian trail, Robertson concealed the main body of his force in the woods near the mouth of Cypress Creek. Soon, they were able to make out what appeared to be cabins alongside the mouth of Spring Creek on the opposite shore.

Six or seven soldiers were sent across the river where they hid in the cane breaks to observe. After determining that this was Oka Kapassa, Colonel Robertson moved his troops across the river and attacked the town. Twenty-six Indians, three French traders and a white woman who had been living with there were killed. The militia burned the village, killed all the hogs and chickens, and buried the three Frenchmen and the white woman. After rewarding the two Chickasaw guides with some of the spoils taken from the village, they returned to their homes in Tennessee.

All was quiet around Nashville for about a month following Robertson's Raid at the Muscle Shoals. Soon, however, small parties of Indians renewed the harassment of the settlers. One of these parties was led by Big Foot from Muscle Shoals.

Bigfoot was quite an oddity among the natives of Muscle Shoals. Whereas the Cherokees and Chickasaws were described as slim and trim and rather handsome in appearance, Big Foot, according to those who saw him, was the fattest and stoutest Indian they had ever seen, and left foot-prints that appeared to be that of a giant from ancient times.

Captain David Shannon from the Cumberland settlement led the second raid to the Muscle Shoals. He came upon Big Foot and his party on the bank of the Tennessee just below the Indian Mound near what was later to become Florence. Some of the Indians were eating while the others were making preparations to cross the river. Shannon's men approached carefully, and at a signal, fired upon the Indians who were eating and immediately charged those who were trying to cross the Tennessee, in hand-to-hand combat.

William Pillow was credited with killing Big Foot. After taking care of one Indian whom he had attacked when the signal was given, he next observed the desperate struggle of a fellow soldier, Luke Anderson, with Big Foot. Much larger and greater in strength, Big Foot had almost wrestled Anderson's gun away from him when Pillow suddenly sprang upon Bigfoot and drove a tomahawk into his skull. Pillow was an uncle of a future General in the Confederate Army, Gideon Pillow.

Witnessing the death of their leader, Bigfoot's warriors fled the scene of battle and were never heard of again.

The victorious Cumberland militiamen made their way back to Tennessee. They had killed the dreaded Creek warrior, Chief Bigfoot. However, it would be another seventeen years before there would be peace in the valleys of the Cumberland and the Tennessee.

UNDERNEATH WILSON LAKE

Hidden under Lake Wilson are interesting geographical features and historical sites. Wilson Dam was completed September 12, 1925. Its backwaters cover 15,930 acres which extend 15.5 miles upriver. Lost underneath are landmarks such as the nineteenth century Muscle Shoals Canal, an engineering accomplishment constructed so as to by-pass the treacherous barriers in the Tennessee River. The park-like grounds of Lock Six, the headquarters for the Canal, were maintained so beautifully that the local people used it for picnics and Sunday afternoon strolls. Even the little steam engine, once used for pulling boats through the nine locks, lies buried under the depths of the lake.

At the time of its completion, Wilson Dam was a pioneer among high-wall dams. Standing 137 feet in height, its backwaters inundated a stretch of the Muscle Shoals known as "the Big Muscle Shoals." This was the worst part of the treacherous fall line where in a distance of some 80 miles between Waterloo and Brown's Ferry the water dropped approximately 200 feet. In 1829 Lieutenant Colonel James Kearney mapped the river at the Muscle Shoals. He depicted eleven dangerous geographical profiles in the fifteen-mile section of the Shoals which now lies under Wilson Lake. These were mostly ragged reefs and sharp drop-offs in the river bed; all were considered almost impossible for navigation except during high-water periods, in late winter and early spring. These barriers were defined as Big Jump, Long Jump, Poor Horse, Grassy Bars, Galloping Water, Eddy, Cox's Run, Rurke Ripple, Cedar Ripple, Brackin Bar, and Flat Rock Bottom. It was said that these names were common knowledge among early river men who plied the Tennessee.

Underneath Wilson Lake are eighteen large and medium-size islands; those upriver from Wilson Dam were: Bainbridge, Crow's Roost, Big Fish Trap, Little Fish Trap, Resting, Little Cow, Big Cow, Turkey Chute. There were two adjoining islands called Sisters, Strones, Coxes, Cedar, Peach Creek, Hog, there were two without names located near the mouth of Blue Water Creek, and Cane Island which is located at Wheeler Dam. Wilson Dam was erected across the western tip of Bainbridge Island; this was later identified as Jackson Island after it was purchased by James Jackson. Resting Island was known by river pilots as a place where they could seek refuge for their crafts before making their final descent over the worst of the Muscle Shoals.

Coxe Island was geographically different from the others. Its head jutted above the water's surface to a height of some eighty feet, making it a natural fortress near the center of the river. This unusual feature was believed to be a volcanic formation. Coxe Island was kidney shaped, about a mile in length and one quarter of a mile in width. There were several springs located on its approximately 180 acres of fertile soil.

Coxe Island was named for Zachariah Coxe who attempted to plant a settlement on this natural fortress in April, 1791. However, he left when a band of Cherokee warriors warned if he did not peacefully withdraw, all in his party would be put to death. Today's lovely and peaceful Wilson Lake conceals a major section of the swift and roaring rapids in the Tennessee River which gave its name to the great Muscle Shoals.

THE BLOCK HOUSE ON COXE'S ISLAND AND ITS LEGACY

Cox Creek Parkway, is perhaps Florence's best known and one of its most traveled thorough-fares. It gets its name from Cox Creek over which the parkway crosses near the busy intersections of Chisholm and Cloverdale Roads. The name given to Cox Creek goes back 200 years to a time when the area was claimed by the Chickasaws, Cherokees, and Creeks. In fact, little is known about the man who, as tradition has it, wrote his own name across an early map as an identification for the then unnamed creek.

Justly or unjustly, the name of Zachariah Coxe was tarnished due to his overly zealous ambitions to own and colonize the Muscle Shoals in the eighteenth century. His land dealings brought him into serious conflict with federal and state authorities as well as the local Indians.

However, Coxe was not the first to show interest in the Shoals. The white speculator's interest in establishing a settlement that can be traced back as early as 1783, when the Muscle Shoals Company was formed and attempts were made to purchase the land from the Cherokees. As the story goes, a group of settlers, led by Valentine Sevier and Stockley Donelson, began a journey down the river not long afterwards. It is not known how far they traveled - some think not much beyond the Alabama line - when they had to turn back because of threats made by the hostile Chickasaws who were vigorously guarding their claim to the Shoals.

Yet, the name of Coxe became engraved in the lore of the Shoals because of the physical evidence left behind after he went away. Not much is known about the life of this man, although there are numerous accounts of his activities in the early territorial documents. A native of Georgia, Coxe was instrumental in organizing the Tennessee Company, one of three corporations receiving grants from the State of Georgia, popularly known as the "Yazoo Land Grants." Most of the information about Coxe can be found in papers related to charges brought against him, as well as events surrounding his eventual arrest and escape.

Coxe was interested in land speculation and in the development of a commercial route between the Tennessee River and Mobile in the period of 1785-1798. His real estate firm induced the State of Georgia in 1789 to grant them three and a half million acres for an agreed price of $46,785. As have developers and promoters before and after, Coxe had his eye mainly on the Muscle Shoals as the centerpiece for his settlement. The Chickasaws, Cherokees, and Creeks were up in arms about these plans. McGilivray of the Creeks seemed even more incensed over what he believed was Coxe's intention to establish another settlement at the mouth of Bear Creek.

Although Coxe advertised his intent to embark on January 10, 1791, for the Muscle Shoals, he apparently was delayed, according to McGilivray, until the following April. Attempts were made all along the journey by the Indians to stop this fleet of armed men and settlers. Upon arriving at the Shoals, the party established a fortification on one of the larger islands in the river.

This site offered some degree of protection. Elk River Shoals guarded it from the east and the impassable Muscle Shoals lay immediately to its west. These settlers named this place, located immediately South of Center Star, "Coxe's Island." Interestingly, this name continued to be used on maps of the Tennessee River as long as the island existed. Coxe's Island is now under the deep back waters of Wilson Lake.

Coxe's first order of business was to erect a large blockhouse on the island. While this was being done, according legend, parties were sent out to explore the land for more suitable dwelling sites. It is believed this was when a previously unknown and uncharted tributary to Cypress Creek: was discovered. Although early maps were available for the river and its tributearies, it is doubtful this stream was shown. In need of a name for identification, according to descendants of early settlers, either Coxe or one of his party inscribed the name "Coxe" on the map.

Coxe's effort to colonize the Shoals failed. He had hardly began when Cherokee Chief Glass appeared with sixty warriors from nearby Melton's Bluff. The Chief warned Coxe if he did not peacefully withdraw, all the party would be put to death. Thus, Coxe reluctantly gathered his people and left. Afterwards, the Indians burned the fortifications. The ruins of this blockhouse became the subject of much speculation among later settlers of Lauderdale County as they wondered who had previously lived there.

Coxe was not one to give up easily. In 1795, Coxe and others purchased all of the land now made up of counties of Colbert,

Lauderdale, Limestone, Franklin, Madison, Jackson, DeKalb, Cherokee, Marshall, and Lawrence, and parts of Marion, Walker, and Blount for $60,000. However, before he could depart with his new colony, Coxe was stopped, this time by the U. S. Army. Both land purchases had been in violation of treaties with the Indians.

Coxe was pursued and eventually arrested at New Orleans around 1798. He soon escaped, and one report says he died as a result of being absolutely "hounded to death." Another more intriguing account tells how his guards helped him escape and he made his way to the Spanish Territory where he was granted asylum by the authorities.

But the name of Zachariah Coxe continues to live in a peaceful stream and in a busy thoroughfare at the center of a settlement *he* had hoped to establish more than two hundred years ago.

CHIEF GLASS

An Indian chief named Thomas Glass was head of a small band of Cherokee warriors at the Muscle Shoals during the latter part of the 18th century. It was said he was closely associated with Chief Doublehead.

Glass was from Lookout Mountain Town where his people knew him as Tauqueto. This chief was especially feared among the white settlers. As a defender of Indian lands his role was of some consequence to the more war-like Cherokee people. The first mention of Thomas Glass is found in the early stories of the Chickamauga Confederacy. This was an alliance made up of approximately 1,000 Cherokee, Creek, and Shawnee tribesmen, along with about 100 whites and blacks who had been adopted into the affiliated tribes. This confederacy was a resistance movement led by the great warrior and prophet, Dragging Canoe, against the intrusion of white settlers on the ancient Indian hunting grounds.

Dragging Canoe's resistance against the whites placed him in opposition to the peace faction of his own people. As a consequence the Chickamauga Confederacy retreated west into the area of preset Chattanooga. Even farther west were other affiliated towns, including Cold Water and Doublehead's Town at the Muscle Shoals. Thomas Glass served as one of Dragging Canoe's lieutenants. On at least one occasion, he led a raiding party of sixty warriors against the Cumberland settlements in middle Tennessee.

Chief Glass was at Melton's Bluff as early as 1791. Now a scenic and isolated ghost town overlooking Wheeler Lake from a high bluff North of Courtland, it took its name from John Melton. Melton used his home as an inn to accommodate the travelers on two wilderness roads that terminated at the bluff. This Irishman, who lived among the Cherokee people, was married to a sister of Chief Doublehead.

Glass is believed to have been a leader of the notorious "pirates" at the Muscle Shoals. These warriors would watch from the high banks of the river as flat boats tried to make their way across the dangerous rapids at Elk Shoals near the present town of Rogersville. Often these boats would be dashed against the numerous projecting rocks or sand bars. When this happened, they were open game to these river pirates who plundered their cargo and sometimes murdered the hapless boatmen.

THE INDIAN FIGHT AT BEAR CREEK

The mouth of Bear Creek, known as Ochappo among the Chickasaws, was the scene of a bloody battle that occurred March 7, 1790, and lasted more than four hours. A mixed group of some 40 warriors, including Cherokees, Creeks, Choctaws, and at least one Shawnee, had assembled there to await the arrival of an American barge under the command of Major John Doughty. Doughty, and his crew of fifteen soldiers and oarsmen, were on a mission to initiate peace among all the Native American Nations South of the Ohio.

Muscle Shoals was at that time, a hotbed of violence. Cherokee Chief Doublehead was conducting raids in Tennessee from his village at the Shoals. The strategic Cherokee fortress at Melton's Bluff was effectively blocking river traffic attempting to pass over the Shoals. The Chickasaws, whose territory overlapped the Cherokees and Creeks at the Shoals, were being terrorized by the Spanish-inspired raids of the vicious people from the Illinois and Wabash country called Kickapoos.

According to Doughty's journal, it took thirteen days of hard rowing up the river to reach an island near the mouth of Bear Creek where he made his camp. A few hours after his arrival, he was approached by four men and a woman in a canoe. Three of the men were Creeks and the fourth was a Shawnee. Doughty, alerted by their suspicious behavior, sent his interpreter, Captain Heart, and an Indian trader named Joseph Maria Francisco Virgo, and his associates, into the vicinity of Bear Creek to collect information and act as messengers.

Unknown to Doughty, the delegation of Native Americans at Bear Creek had been persuaded by the Creek representatives to attack and destroy the American peace envoy. Plans were made to invite the Americans to a feast, and at a pre-arranged signal, the warriors were to kill Doughty and his men with tomahawks concealed under their blankets. To the credit of Cherokee Chief Sawai - who was sick in camp - he made a strong effort to prevent this from happening.

Through the alertness of Major Doughty, however, this deception failed, leading instead to a fierce naval battle in the middle of the Tennessee River. On March 7th, as Doughty headed toward the mouth of Bear Creek, he was confronted by four large canoes, each of which had hoisted a white flag. Acting with caution, Doughty allowed their leader, Shawnee Chief Popoquan, and three of his men, to come aboard the American barge for a discussion which lasted about an hour.

Shortly thereafter, while Doughty was attempting to maneuver his barge across the river, he and his men came under deadly fire from those aboard the four canoes. In his journal, Doughty described his escape by floating down the river during which time "they pursued us for about four hours."

In the battle, five of Major Doughty's men were killed and six were wounded. It was later estimated by the Indian trader, Vigo, that eight of the warriors were either killed or wounded.

Thus, the attempt by President George Washington and his Secretary of War, Henry Knox, to initiate an end to war and strife among the Native Americans in this part of the Tennessee Valley came to naught. It would take several more years before there would be peace at the Muscle Shoals.

7 CHIEF TUSCUMBIA

Old Chief Tuscumbia became a legend at the Muscle Shoals. He was one of the few inhabitants of the area when the first white settlers arrived. His name in the Chickasaw language was "Tashka Ambi", or "Tashkambi", meaning "the warrior who kills." It was the English, Scots and Irish who later changed the spelling to "Tuscumbia."

Although he wore the title of Chief, he has never been listed among the principal chiefs of his people. One source in Mississippi

> The town of Tuscumbia and the Tuscumbia Mountain in Northwest Alabama as well as the Tuscumbia River in Northern Mississippi were named for Chief Tashka Ambi.

refer-red to him as one of the priesthood, being labeled as "Chief Rainmaker of the Chickasaw Tribe".

Chief Tashka Ambi was a contemporary of other notable Indians who lived at the Muscle Shoals. Chickasaw Chief George Colbert operated a ferry and an inn a few miles west of Tuscumbia on the Tennessee River at the crossing of the Natchez Trace. Cherokee Chief Doublehead lived across the river in what later was to become Lauderdale County, and Chiefs Bigfoot and Glass were at one time or another in the Colbert County area.

The Chickasaw Nation, with a population that ranged between an estimated 3,500 to 4,500, was small in comparison to its neighbors, the Cherokees, Choctaws and Creeks. The early domain of the Chickasaws included Northern Mississippi, Eastern Tennessee, Southwestern Kentucky and a small section of Northwest Alabama.

The Chickasaws' closest cultural affinity was with the Choctaws, and it is believed that in more ancient times they were an integral part of the Choctaw tribe. The Chickasaw and Choctaw language, except for dialect differences, were the same. Their language, known as the Muskhogean, was described by early settlers as very agreeable to the ear, courteous, gentle and musical.

At the time Chief Tashka Ambi lived at the Big Spring in what would become Tuscumbia. The cap-ital of the Chickasaws was in Mississippi at Old Pontotoc, or Long Town, near what was to become Tupelo.

How the Chickasaws came to this part of the Southeast is a basic part of their early religious belief. According to the tradition of their elders, their original home at some remote historic time was in the land of the setting sun; which was probably in Mexico or Central America. Each generation, it was said, was instructed in the long and difficult search for the homeland ordained by their deities. Their guide was an oracular pole, carried on each day's march by the tribe's holy men.

Each night the priests placed the pole upright in the ground. During the night, the pole would, shift about and the direction to which it had shifted served as a compass to guide the new day's march. Almost without fail they moved toward the rising sun and eventually crossed the Mississippi and continued eastward until they reached the Tennessee River.

They journeyed as far as what is now Madison County, Alabama, and at that point the pole remained erect. With great rejoicing the tribe believed they had found the "Promised Land." They cleared their fields, planted corn and built settlements. After a time, however, the pole leaned westward and the Chickasaws abandoned their settlements and marched in the direction from whence they had come. In the Tombigbee high-lands of Northeast Mississippi the pole once again remained erect, and this, their new promised land, was where they were when the white settlers came into the territory.

When the white people made their first contact, Chief Tuscumbia was living with a small group of his people at the Muscle Shoals. His brother Jack lived near what was to become Corinth, Mississippi.

Colonel James Robertson of Nashville led a raid in June 1787 to the mouth of Spring Creek. At that time he burned the Indian village known as Oka Kapassa and the French Trading Post that had thrived there for some time. Twenty-six Indians, three French traders, and a white woman were killed.

Robertson had learned from the Chickasaws that the warriors from this village at the Muscle Shoals, mainly Creeks and Cherokees, were the ones responsible for the raids against the white settlers in Middle Tennessee.

Chief Tashka Ambi was a young warrior at that time, it is doubtful he had any connections with the people at Oka Kapassa. However, one historian, in writing about this era at the Muscle Shoals, had this to say about Chief Tuscumbia:

> "The settlements were continually being harassed by Indians from all quarters, but the Indians' particular stronghold was the territory along the Tennessee River and to the South of Tennessee. One of the particularly spiteful chiefs was named Tuscumbia who lived at the great spring where the city of Tuscumbia is now located."

It was about this time in the late 1780's that Chief Tuscumbia married Im Mi, whose full name was Im Mi Ah Key. There was a strict rule among the Chickasaws that a brave had to go outside his home clan to find a wife. It is believed Tuscumbia found his bride in the eastern part of the nation. It was also not uncommon among the Chickasaws for a brave to have more than one wife at the same time, especially if there were a number of sisters in the bride's family. Im Mi apparently had no sisters therefore, from all accounts; she remained Chief Tuscumbia's only wife as long as he lived.

The Chickasaw marriage came about after the brave declared his matrimonial intentions by sending the young lady a small present. "If she accepted the gift," they were considered engaged. The marriage ceremony was a gala event in the village and quite different from the traditions brought into the land by the white settlers. James Adair, who lived among the Chickasaws, described the proceedings as follows:

> "the groom divides an ear of corn in two pieces before witnesses. He keeps one of the pieces and presents his bride with the other half. After accepting the corn, or sometimes a deer's foot, the bride then proceeds to present her new husband with some cakes of bread that she has prepared for the marriage occasion".

When Michael Dickson and his family landed at Muscle Shoals in 1815, they found Chief Tuscumbia and Im Mi to be an amiable couple. Dickson was able to persuade the chief to sell him the site of the City of Tuscumbia, plus all the land between the Big Spring and Tuscumbia Mountain to the South, and all the land to the Tennessee River on the North, for the amazing price of five dollars and two pole axes. This became known as "the Tomahawk Claim." After the Federal Government acquired the Indian lands following the Treaty of 1816, they allowed Dickson two lots in the town of Tuscumbia for his claim.

The city that later was to be named for Chief Tuscumbia was incorporated December 20, 1820 as Cold Water. Six months later the name was changed to Big Spring, and on December 31, 1822, it was changed a third time to Tuscumbia. There is a legend that the citizens were asked to select either the name "Annie", in honor of the infant daughter of Michael Dickson, who was the first white child born at that place, or the name "Tuscumbia" in honor of the old chief who was still living in the community. The name Tuscumbia won by a majority of one vote, and the Chickasaw chieftain was so pleased that he presented little Annie with a tiny pair of moccasins.

Sometime after 1822, Chief Tuscumbia and his wife, Im Mi, moved back to his old home some nine miles South of the present city of Corinth, near the Danville community. Here Chief Tuscumbia built a small cabin on land that adjoined his brother Jack's property. The Chief spent the remaining years of his life as a farmer; it was said, using a primitive plow drawn behind a pinto pony.

Chief Tuscumbia died about the year 1834. A grave was dug under the couch, inside the house, where he had died. They washed his body, anointed his head with oil, painted his face red, and dressed him in his best clothes. The body was placed in a sitting position facing west, and his personal effects, including his gun, ammunition, pipe, tobacco and a supply of corn, were placed alongside the body in the grave. The mourning for the chief involved extinguishing the fire in his house, removing all ashes, and starting a new fire. His widow, Im Mi, according to Chickasaw tradition, wept over his grave just before sunup and sundown for a month.

In December 1836, a neighbor, Ruffin Coleman, bought Im Mi's land for $820; she had been granted this farm by the Treaty of 1834. In 1838 Im Mi and her children were forced to follow the Trail of Tears to Oklahoma with the other Chickasaws.

Chief Tuscumbia's grave near Danville, Mississippi, was only a short distance from the Tuscumbia River that bears his name. In 1838, Im Mi's old homeplace was sold again, this time to Hesekiah Balch Mitchell, for the price of $2,000. Mitchell built his home, which became known as "The White House" on the high ground where he and his son, Lyman, had earlier attended the funeral of Chief Tuscumbia. Not wishing to build over the old chief, he removed Tuscumbia's body to another location, and in the passing of time, the exact site of the second grave has been lost.

But the name of Tuscumbia will not soon be forgotten, for there is a river in Mississippi, and a city and a mountain in Alabama named for him. They speak softly of the noble warrior who lived among these lands before the white man came to take it from a proud people known as the Chickasaws.

AN HISTORIC ABORIGINAL VILLIAGE AT COLDWATER

The early Indian history of Tuscumbia is intriguing. Not much is known, but what little is discernible leaves the historian with even more unanswerable questions. The late 18th century village of Oka Kapassa, or "Coldwater," was located about one mile west of the Big Spring at the mouth of Spring Creek. It was established by the Chickamaugas, a rebel branch of the Cherokee Nation. Yet its name came not from the Cherokees, but from the language of the Chickasaws.

The war-like Chickamaugas had pulled away from the main body of the Cherokees about 1777 under their fierce and unrelenting leader, Dragging Canoe. Two years later, their towns were destroyed by Col. Isaac Shelby. Dragging Canoe, not to be undone, merely moved his people to five new locations: Lookout Mountain, Crow Town, Running Water Town, Nickajack and Long Island Town. Oka Kapassa is believed to have come into being during the American Revolution as the most westward outpost of the Cherokees. Its purpose was to protect the supply base in the Muscle Shoals. These goods were being supplied by the French at Detroit. Boats came by way of the Wabash and up the Tennessee as far as the Shoals where, due to the shallows and rapids, they could go no farther. The cargo was unloaded at Oka Kapassa and transported by horses and wagons to five Chickamauga towns along the upper Tennessee.

Initially, about 100 French traders made their way to Oka Kapassa. Thirty of these white people remained as part of the Indian community. They brought their own bodyguards, made up of Shawnees and Delawares. One document in the Spanish Archives, dated Jan. 23, 1787, complains that the French had at that time more supplies in Muscle Shoals than all the Southern Indians could buy in three years.

According to a number of accounts, the houses in these villages were dirty flea ridden, unsightly and uncomfortable. At this period of history, these were log dwellings with makeshift roofs and dirt floors. The furnishings consisted of bunks that were used as beds and a place to sit. A fireplace was in the center of the room from which smoke made its escape through a hole in the roof. Except during the worst of weather, all cooking was done on the outside and not inside the cabin. Characteristically, the Indian was an outdoor person. His home served merely as a shelter from the weather, a place to sleep at night, and a place to depart from as early as possible the next morning.

Another element to the enigma of Oka Kapassa concerns its likely antiquity; it is believed by some historians that the Chickamaugas were not its original inhabitants. Based upon its name and the Hutchins map of 1760, it is thought that it may have been settled first by the Chickasaws.

Judging from its location among bountiful waters from Tuscumbia's Big Spring, it may even have been the home of the Shawnees or Creeks who preceded the Chickasaws into Northwest Alabama; or maybe the Yuchi who were on the Tennessee River before 1700 could have lived there. One could speculate even further back among the historic Indians. Indeed, it would be too farfetched to conjecture that the Siovans, who left the Great Lakes in some remote pre-Columbian time to become probably the oldest inhabitants of the South, could have been the first to establish their home at Tuscumbia.

CHIEF TUSCUMBIA'S INN ON THE NATCHEZ TRACE

One of Florence's closest Tennessee neighbors is Cypress Inn, which practically straddles the Alabama/Tennessee line a few miles North of Cloverdale on Alabama Highway 157.

Cypress Inn traces its history back to about 1805, when the Chickasaw Nation agreed to create three stands North of the Tennessee River "for the accommodation of travelers on the Natchez Trace."

112

Cypress Inn was originally known as Toscomby's Stand. Toscomby is believed to have been the same Chickasaw Chief for whom the city of Tuscumbia was named in 1822.

Toscomby's Stand is 16 miles North of Colbert's Ferry on the Natchez Trace. For that reason, the inn was sometimes, referred to as "The 16-Mile House."

One traveler noted in 1811 that this was the Northern most settlement of the Chickasaw people at the Muscle Shoals.

The accommodations consisted of several primitive buildings. The main structure, known as the Kentucky House, was used for eating and entertaining. A number of nearby outbuildings were for overnight lodging. The attached lean-tos were for horses and guest over-flows as needed.

In the Treaty of 1816, the Chickasaw Nation gave up title to most of their land, including the area North of the Tennessee River. Wayne County was first created by an act of the Tennessee Legislature in 1817; it was necessary for this act to be passed again in 1819 because of a technical problem.

However, by this time, Chief Tuscumbia was living near the Big Spring near present day Tuscumbia, where Michael Dickson, an early settler, first met the chief in 1815 or, perhaps, in 1817.

According to one source, there was a powder mill in the Cypress Inn area of Wayne County as early as 1810. This pioneer enterprise may have been operated by the Chickasaws or by early white settlers for the Chickasaw people.

It is not known when the name of the old Toscomby's Inn was changed to Cypress Inn. This may have occurred 1817, when the early white settlers began moving into the area. The new name, Cypress Inn, was obviously chosen because of the nearby Cypress Creek, which flows through the community. According to tradition, groves of great cypress trees once grew alongside this picturesque Alabama stream.

A post office was established at Cypress Inn on May 18, 1839. William Duncan, who operated the postal service out of his home, was appointed, the first postmaster. At one time, there were several general stores, a grist mill and blacksmith shop in the community. In the latter part of the 19th century, Cypress Inn was also the location of a cotton gin and cobbler's shop.

Among the earliest settlers was John L. Lindsey. At the age of 15, John served with his father and three uncles in the Carolina Militia during the Revolutionary War. It is believed that this old soldier was buried in the Cooper Cemetery alongside Cooper Branch in Cypress Inn. Vandals recently destroyed some of the graves in this pioneer cemetery.

8 "White Path" The Protector of Indian Lands

Colonel Return Jonathan Meigs (1740-1823)
Cherokee Indian Agent

WHITE PATH THE PROTECTOR OF INDIAN LANDS AT THE MUSCLE SHOALS

As early as 1801, and until his death in 1823, the name of Colonel Return Jonathan Meigs appears in countless government documents pertaining to Indians and treaties in Tennessee, and North of the Tennessee River in Alabama. Probably no single individual had more affect upon the eventual removal of the Native Americans from the Muscle Shoals than did Colonel Meigs. By the same token, no man contributed more to the peaceful settlement of North Alabama than Meigs, who was called "White Path" by the Cherokees.

Numerous legends of the actions of this relentless protector of the Indians' rights are substantiated at least in part by papers and letters of early settlers as well as his rather sketchy manuscripts in the National Archives at Washington. From about 1810 to 1814, a contingent of U.S. troops was stationed at Fort Hampton on the east bank of Elk River near Rogersville, Alabama, to carry out Meigs' policy of keeping the illegal white squatters out of what would become Lauderdale and Limestone Counties. Most of these evictions occurred at Elk River, Shoal Creek, Blue Water Creek, and Cypress Creek.

On more than one occasion Colonel Meigs personally negotiated with Chief George Colbert at the ferry on the Natchez Trace. Colbert did not trust Meigs, who during the same period was a friend and ally of Colbert's father-in-law, Cherokee Chief Doublehead.

The name of Return Jonathan Meigs covers a span of American history for more than 150 years. The first record of the use of this unusual family name begins with Return Jonathan Meigs, Sr., of Connecticut, who married Elizabeth Hamlin. They became the parents of Return Jonathan Meigs, Jr., who was to become known as White Path among the Cherokees in Tennessee.

A story is told that when Vincent Jonathan Meigs first called on his future wife that her father refused to allow him to entertain the young lady. As the rejected Jonathan was leaving, the father changed his mind. Excitedly, the young bride-to-be ran to the door and cried out "Return Jonathan, Return!" Thus, they named their first child "Return Jonathan Meigs."

The senior Return Jonathan Meigs was a hat maker by trade, and served in the Connecticut General Assembly. He was descended from Vincent Meigs who emigrated from Dorsetshire, England, about 1635.

White Path, or Return Jonathan Meigs, Jr., was born December 17, 1740, at Middletown, Connecticut. In 1772, Governor Trumbull of the Connecticut Colony appointed him as a lieutenant in the Sixth Connecticut Regiment. Within two years he was elevated to the rank of captain.

Meigs became quite a legend during the Revolutionary war. After the Battle of Lexington, he marched his company to Boston and participated in the defense of that city. Later, as major, he joined General Benedict Arnold in the expedition to Quebec. He was among the first of the Americans to scale the walls of the city, at which time he was captured and later exchanged. Meigs kept a diary during this ill-fated campaign. It was written with ink that he made by mixing powder and water in the palm of his hand.

After his release from the British stockade, Meigs was promoted to the rank of lieutenant colonel and awarded a ceremonial sword by a grateful Congress for his bravery at Sag Harbor. According to the military citation, Meigs, with some 160 men from General Parson's forces, crossed at Long Island using 13 whaleboats as a convoy protected by two armed sloops. Upon reaching the shore Meigs marched to Sag Harbor with so much speed that he completely surprised the unsuspecting British garrison. In quick order Meigs burned eleven or twelve English ships, destroyed a large quantity of military stores, killed several at the garrison, and took 90 prisoners, without the loss of a man under his command. This amazing victory occurred at a time when the American people were in need of a boost in their efforts to continue the struggle against Great Britain.

Following the Battle of Sag Harbor, Meigs was promoted to colonel and placed in command of the Sixth Connecticut Infantry. Known as the "Leather Cap Regiment", it participated in all principal engagements along the Hudson under its new commander.

Meigs was cited the second time by Congress "for raising the morale of the American Army". This time his citation read that he was one of the first under General Anthony Wayne to storm the fort at Stony Point.

Colonel Meigs received a letter of commendation from General Washington in May 1780 in recognition of his prompt action in suppressing a mutiny among the Connecticut troops.

This gallant officer was one of Americans sent to defend West Point after the high treason of Benedict Arnold came to light.

When the war ended, Meigs received an appointment as a surveyor, for the Ohio Company. This opened new doors in the unsettled west. In April 1788, he landed at the mouth of the Muskingum with a small group, of New England settlers. Meigs was credited with drawing up a code of rules that were adopted by the colony and posted on a large oak tree near the center of the settlement.

Colonel Return Meigs married Joanna Winborn in 1764. After her death in 1773, he married Rising Fawn, an American Indian.

One of the several children of Colonel Meigs was Return Jonathan Meigs, III. He was a graduate of Yale University, Governor of Ohio, Chief Justice of the Ohio Supreme Court, Commander of Troops and Militia in the St. Charles District of Louisiana, U.S. Senator, and, in 1814, was appointed Postmaster General of the United States.

The fourth generation family heir to be named Return Jonathan Meigs was a grandson of the Cherokee Indian Agent by the same name who was called White Path by the Indians. This fourth generation Return Jonathan Meigs lived some 90 years and, like his forefathers, accumulated a number of achievements as an attorney and as a writer. He became a controversial figure in Tennessee during the Civil War as a result of his strong ties with the Union. Because of this he moved to New York, and in 1863 received an appointment as Clerk of the Supreme Court of the District of Columbia.

Colonel Return Jonathan Meigs, Jr. the "White Path" among the Cherokees was appointed as Indian Agent to that Nation in 1801. In 1804, 1805 and 1807 he was commissioned to negotiate treaties, and in 1808 was granted authority to negotiate a convention between the State of Tennessee and the Cherokee Nation. Because of these commissions Meigs was instrumental in the treaties between the Indians and the white man that eventually led to the settlement and development of the area North of the Tennessee River in Alabama.

As a result of complaints from both the Chickasaw and Cherokee Nations following the death of Chief Doublehead in 1807, Colonel Meigs implemented a policy to remove the white settlers from the lands in and around the Muscle Shoals. He eventually had to resort to the use of U.S. troops. This was not an easy task, and its consequences resulted in extreme hardships among those evicted. Yet, Meigs' policy laid the ground-work that brought about peaceful negotiations with both Indian groups. These series of treaties, finalized in 1816, opened up the territory for permanent settlement by the white pioneers.

There was much resentment in the Tennessee Valley against Colonel Meigs by practically all of the earliest white settlers, and, especially by the Chickasaw Nation who saw him as an enemy. However, he was admired and trusted among the Cherokees whom he served for many years as their "govern-ment agent." The final act of his life was in service to those whom he, in turn, loved and respected. The story goes that on a cold winter night at the Hiwassee Garrison, Colonel Meigs learned that a visiting chief, who was aged and not well, had no place to sleep. Meigs gave him his bed, and moved into a tent. As a result of this exposure to the elements, Meigs, then 82 years of age, contracted pneumonia and died January 28, 1823.

CHICKASAW CONFERENCE AT CAMPBELL'S FERRY

On August 12, 1816, General John Coffee met at Camp-bell's Ferry with a number of Chickasaw chiefs. This ferry, located at the old Bambridge Crossing known now as the Kendale Gardens Subdivision, had been in operation as early as 1804. In early days it was the major crossing place of the Tennessee River at the Muscle Shoals. At the time of this 1816 conference, the future site of Florence was in the midst of an old forest made up mostly of large white oaks. Both Coffee and Jackson referred to it as "the woods" as late as 1817.

Coffee had recently been appointed by President James Madison as Surveyor of Indian Lands. His duties were to survey the former Creek lands that had been ceded to the United

States at the 1814 Treaty of Fort Jackson. Coffee immediately ran into boundary line problems with the neighboring Indian tribes. These disputes became so heated that General Jackson called for twenty-five mounted militia to protect the new Surveyor of Indian lands. At the same time Coffee wrote Chief George Colbert, leader of the Chickasaw tribe, that if his people attempted to interrupt his work they would be promptly punished. His initial attempt to resolve these boundary line problems was by calling for conferences with the various tribes.

Coffee invited the Chickasaw representatives to meet with him on the Tennessee River at Campbell's Ferry. Here, Coffee and his commissioners met on the appointed day with Colonel William Cooke, Chickasaw Agent, along with a number of prominent chiefs. After being entertained with a dinner at the ferry, they were moved back a mile from the river where a camp was set up to begin deliberations.

The Chickasaw people came well prepared for their confrontation with Coffee. They had a letter signed by President George Washington that had given them a clear title to the land in dispute. They also drew up a statement setting forth their claims and demanded that Coffee's work to establish the boundary line be stopped. Realizing the legality of the Chickasaw claim, Coffee and his commissions agreed the following day to abandon their survey until further notice.

These boundary land disputes were filially resolved later in the year. The Chickasaw people were given an annuity amounting to $12,000, along with $4,000 for improvements. The Cherokee annuity was $6,000 with $5,000 for improvements. The last of these treaties was with the Choctaw Nation. They settled for annuity of $6,000 to be paid over a period of twenty years along with an immediate delivery of merchandise totaling $10,000.

Following these conferences, Coffee was able to write to his wife Polly, "that we have once more obtained the country conquered by arms...".

The Surveyor of Indians Lands resumed his work of running the boundary lines on November 29,1816.

It is said that Coffee owned surveying instruments equal to any in the whole country. His task was now made easier in that the treaties provided for a delegation from each tribe to help determine the boundary lines. The actual marking of these boundaries began on December 17 and was completed in little more than a month.

General John Coffee was later appointed Surveyor General, which allowed him to survey the Southern line of Tennessee and the boundary between Alabama and Mississippi. He had come a long way from the 1816 Conference with the Chickasaw chiefs at Campbell's Ferry.

DUTCH LANDING

Dutch Landing lies hidden under the backwaters of Wilson Dam. During the latter 1700's and early 1800's, this place, South of Elgin in East Lauderdale County, served the local Cherokee Indians and the earliest white settlers. Before steamboat days, this was the nearest port for flatboats and keelboats above the Muscle Shoals.

Dutch Landing was one of the few natural ports in North Alabama. As the Tennessee River formed its bed through this part of the state, its shore lines were normally rugged and inaccessible with high and steep bluffs. Dutch Landing was one of a few accessible places in and among these jagged water edges at the head of the dreaded river obstacle called the Muscle Shoals. The location of Dutch Landing was almost level with the water. This feature, mindful of the lowlands of Holland, is thought to have been the origin of its foreign-sounding name.

Dutch Landing lay between the mouths of Blue Water and Second Creeks. To the west of Blue Water are the high Double-head Bluffs. On the opposite bank of the river is what was once known as Green Bluff. East of Dutch Landing is the high banks that now serve as anchors for Wheeler Dam. The curved hill to the North of what was once Dutch Landing led to the plateau where the community of Elgin is located.

Prior to the coming of the white settlers, the Cherokees made use of the Tennessee as a means of transportation. All of their major towns were located along the banks of the river and its tributaries. Doublehead's Village was near the mouth of Blue Water Creek. It depended upon nearby Dutch Landing as its port for supplies arriving periodically from the larger Cherokee towns in East Tennessee. Chief Doublehead became personally interested in this landing as a means of commercial development. In 1802, he requested the United States Indian Agent near the Hiawassee River "to have me a boat built. I want a good keelboat some 30 to 35 feet in length and 7 feet wide. I want her for the purpose of descending the river to Orleans and back I want her to be light and well calculated to stem the stream. I am determined to buy the produce of this place and the return by water."

Following the establishment of two private reserves for Chief Doublehead in 1806, he and others formed a company to lease thousands of acres to white settlers between Elk River and Cypress Creek. River crafts brought in a number of these settlers. These people also depended upon river transportation for their supplies and goods.

Dutch Landing was one of four ports above the Muscle Shoals in the Great Bend of the Tennessee River. Ditto's Landing, South of Huntsville, was established by John Ditto around 1804. Brown's Ferry, the location of TVA's Nuclear Plant near Athens, was the second ferry founded by a Cherokee named John Brown. His first river-crossing enterprise was in Tennessee near Chattanooga. Later, he moved down the river to Limestone County. He is believed to have been the Colonel John Brown who was married to the widow Nancy Allison. Nancy was a sister to Bartley and Joshua Cox who settled near Brown's Ferry in 1818. The other early flatboat and keelboat ports above the Muscle Shoals in the Great Bend were Dutch Landing and Lamb's Ferry. The latter, South of Rogersville, was established around 1816 by John Lamb and his son who moved there from Indian Creek in Giles County, Tennessee.

Amid the peaceful and placid twentieth-century TVA lakes it is difficult to realize the awesome appearance of the Muscle Shoals, which in a distance of less than thirty-eight miles dropped almost 138 feet. This part of the Tennessee River was filled with dangerous rapids, swirls, sinks, shallows, reefs, falls, islands, and sandbars. During the summer and fall months it was almost impossible for boats to pass over the Shoals. Those pilots who crossed it during high-water times did so at certain risks.

Yet, it was the Muscle Shoals that for all practical purposes, divided this mighty stream of water into two rivers: the Upper Tennessee and the Lower Tennessee. It was this great barrier between the two rivers which gave both birth and life to the primitive port called Dutch Landing. Following the arrival of the steamboats, this place soon lost its usefulness. After the completion of the Muscle Shoals Canal, there was some shipping of cotton and grain from this site. Its final demise however, came when Wilson Dam was completed in 1925, and its slowly-rising backwaters erased forever the lowland that had once been called Dutch Landing.

FORT HAMPTON

Fort Hampton was an early nineteenth century army post located about seven miles east of Rogersville and near the Elk River in what is now Limestone County. The main purpose of this frontier outpost was to protect Indian lands from white intruders.

In those days the boundary between the Cherokee and Chickasaw is said to have overlapped near the community of Center Star in Lauderdale County. The Cherokee's ceded their claims to this land north of the Tennessee River in 1806, although a large reserve between Elk River and Cypress Creek had been set aside for Chief Doublehead. Almost immediately this local chief began leasing land to settlers. By 1810 there were approximately 200 white families living here.

The Chickasaw, using rough calculations, estimated between four to five thousand white people were living at that time on their tribal lands in Mississippi and Alabama, including these families on the Doublehead Reserve. They were incensed and demanded for the federal government to take the necessary action to push these people back across the line into Tennessee. On June 12, 1809, Colonel Return Jonathan Meigs, the Cherokee Indian Agent who had won his laurels during the American Revolution, reported that his soldiers had marched over 400 miles in a campaign that took 51 days to evict 201

125

families from the Chickasaw lands. However, a number of these people returned to their crude cabins, along with new settlers. The Chickasaw's accused Colonel Meigs of allowing this to happen. Thus, the pressure became so great that Fort Hampton was built in June, 1810, as a permanent military base. It was quickly manned by soldiers who staged their first raids from the fort in June of that year. Another sweep across the territory was made by these soldiers in June 1811.

Although there were few noted exceptions, the troops at Fort Hampton dealt roughly with the settlers. More than 65 years later, James McCallum told about these raids. The soldiers, he said, cut down their corn with large butcher knives, burned their fences and houses, and forced them back across the line into Tennessee. These incidents occurred all over East Lauderdale County from the Elk River to the banks of Cypress Creek west of present Florence.

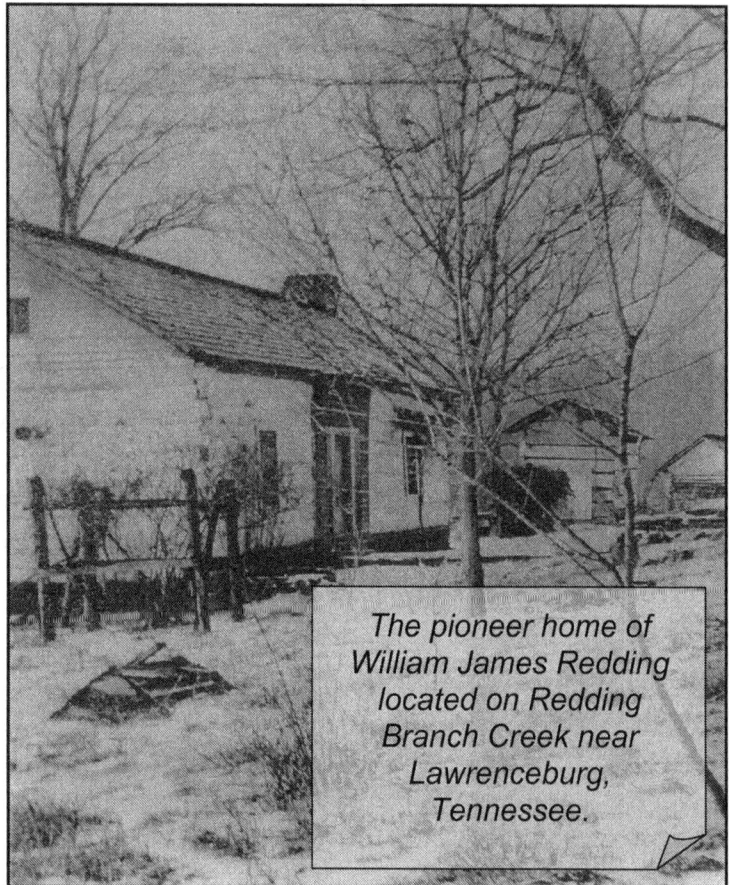

The pioneer home of William James Redding located on Redding Branch Creek near Lawrenceburg, Tennessee.

Mail to this outpost was delivered every other week, sometimes under difficult circumstances. A number of frontier roads were established in and out of this military base which made it the center of activities in the untamed wilderness west of Huntsville. One road led to Mooresville, another to Elkton, Tennessee. A third, Mitchell's Trace, tied Fort Hampton to Fort Mitchell on the Chattahoochee River. In the October 19, 1813, edition of *The Nashville Whig* a report was made as to the activities of Andrew Jackson's Army which indicates that Fort Hampton, at least temporally, saw service during the War of 1812. In 1817 Fort Hampton became the county seat of Elk County, which a year later was carved into Lauderdale and Limestone Counties. By 1821, this post had fallen into disuse and decay.

Old Fort Hampton is remembered today only through a few faded records that, too, have all but disappeared in the passing of time. Yet, this outpost played an important role in the transition of this ancient home of the Cherokee and Chickasaw into what has become the crossroads, communities, villages, towns, and cities of Limestone and Lauderdale counties in Northwest Alabama.

NAVIGATING THE MUSCLE SHOALS

"When we approached them they had a dreadful appearance to those who had never seen them before."

The writer, Colonel John Donelson, was describing the Muscle Shoals from aboard his flagship "Adventure" in what has been labeled by a well-known Tennessee historian as "the most famous voyage in the annals of the pioneers."

The Muscle Shoals, prior to the building of Wilson, Wheeler, and Pickwick Dams, was a dreaded and dangerous barrier in the Tennessee River. In a short span between Elk River and Florence, a distance of almost forty miles, the river dropped a little over 137 feet, creating rushing cascades of waterfalls, along with sinks, sand bars, shallows, rapids, and a large number of islands of varying sizes.

Perhaps one of the best early descriptions of the Muscle Shoals was penned in 1818 by America's first female reporter, Anne Newport Royall: "...a most sublime picture...the noise it produced by the water rushing over the rocks was tremendous...We saw a boat hung on the rocks about the middle of the stream, and many persons around it on the rocks, endeavoring to get it off; the waves and white caps were dashing furiously around them..."

Nancy Adair Redding at her spinning wheel.

It was a cold day in March 1780 when Colonel Donelson and his colony of emigrants arrived in Northwest Alabama. Three days before Christmas in 1779, they had left what is now Kingsport, Tennessee.

His fleet of flatboats had already passed through almost unbearable and almost indescribable hardships, including losses of lives and essential property, as they made their way through the bloody gantlet of Cherokee Chief Dragging Canoes' towns below present Chattanooga. Now, they had arrived at what was considered the most dangerous obstacle in the river, the great Muscle Shoals.

"Here we did not know how soon we would be bashed to pieces," wrote the Colonel. "Our boats frequently dragged on the bottom, and appeared constantly in danger of striking; they warped as much as in a rough sea. But, by the hand of Providence, we are now preserved from this danger also." Two days later, near the Creek town of Coldwater, now Tuscumbia. Five men were wounded by Indians who were firing from the South bank of the river.

Colonel John Donelson and his crew of what would become the "first families of Nashville," safely made their way across the Shoals and up the Ohio and Cumberland Rivers to their middle Tennessee destination.

Even before Donelson, a few parties of emigrants bound for Natchez or the Illinois country had made the dangerous crossing of the Muscle Shoals. After Donelson, these attempts slowed to a thin trickle. Some were successful while others failed.

One such failure occurred in 1794 when William Scott and his party of thirty-three emigrants were overtaken by the Indians as they were attempting to cross over the hazardous Muscle Shoals. All the white people in Scott's party were killed and the African-American slaves on board the boats were taken prisoner.

William Scott's ill-fated attempt to navigate his boats over the dangerous and troubled waters near Florence is regarded as the worst of river tragedies at the Muscle Shoals. It perhaps, resulted in one of its bloodiest massacres.

9 Early Settlers Who Lived Among The Indians

Captain Henry Davis Allen (1782- 1873), one of Lauderdale's first settlers.
(Photograph courtesy of Fred Johnson, author of I'M FROM LEXINGTON, published in 1989.)

LAUDERDALE COUNTY'S PIONEER HOUGH FAMILY

Early settlers found a number of Indian trails that criss-crossed the Muscle Shoals. Hough Road was originally one of these paths. It connected the old Doublehead Trace, which ran from Middle Tennessee to Cherokee chief Doublehead's Village near the mouth of Blue Water Creek, to an early river crossing at the mouth of Cypress Creek. This trail later became the western link for the Pulaski Pike prior to the coming of the railroads.

Hough Road bears the name of an early pioneer family. It is said that John Reuben Hough left Chesterfield County, South Carolina, during the early part of the 19th century and joined what may have been a trading expedition that was traveling down the Tennessee River. Some accounts tell that, upon reaching the Shoals, Hough liked what he saw, and remained here to live among the local Native Americans.

Smallwood Plantation, the early log home built by John Reeves Hough, once stood near Interstate of U.S. Highway 72 and County Road 27 east of Florence. (Smallwood Family shown in photo about 1911.)

He later acquired two large tracts of land in 1818 and 1822. One was near the junction of Shoal and Indian Camp Creeks. The second tract was near today's Goose Shoals Bridge over

Shoal Creek. The eldest son of John Reuben Hough was John Reeves Hough. His large two-story framed house stood for many years at the intersection of U.S. Highway 72 East and what is now County Road 27. This intersection led to a pioneer Tennessee River crossing known as Campbell's Ferry. County Road 27 was laid out in 1819 as the Northern part of the old Byler Road, Alabama's first state highway. John Reeves Hough died in 1849 and is buried near his home site in the Hough-Smith Cemetery, also known as the Jones-Hill Cemetery.

The second son of John Reuben Hough was Joseph Hough who was born in 1801 in South Carolina. Joseph acquired large tracts of land on both sides of Shoal Creek at the crossing of the early Indian trail which has became known as Hough Road.

In 1859, Joseph Hough came into possession of what is known today as the Tate's Spring Estate. This had been the pioneer home of Benjamin Seixas and, consequently became known locally as "The Seixas." This has been home of the descendants of Joseph Hough for more than 150 years.

The widow Annie Hough's plantation was located on Hough Road near the modern Books-A-Million, store on Cox Creek Parkway. On, January 25, 1864 a fierce skirmish occurred at Widow Hough's place between a unit of the U.S. 72nd Indiana Cavalry and part of the Confederate Colonel William A. Johnson's Regiment.

After the Civil War, a number of African-American families established Houghtown near the intersection of Hough and Middle Roads. Two nearby cemeteries served as the final resting place of a number of these families. One is known as the Huss Cemetery.

The history of Hough Road reaches across a number of centuries to include the presence of Native Americans, the coming of the early white settlers and their dependence upon the river for goods and services. Its history also records the struggles faced by the local African-Americans as they began a new way of life following their emancipation from slavery.

EARLY SETTLERS

The Chickasaw agent reported in 1810 that from 4,000 to 5,000 white intruders were scattered in settlements on Chickasaw lands. It is believed that more than half of these people were living in the present counties of Lauderdale and Limestone.

Conditions were primitive. These families had traveled over almost non-existing Indian trails and crossed hazardous rivers and streams at the risk of life and property. They came without the most ordinary conveniences, bringing only what could be carried on their backs or packed on their animals. They carved a homestead in the wilderness without even the basic utensils and tools. They depended upon their own "household industry" for the weaving of cloth for clothing and the tanning of leather for coats and shoes. Food and shelter were their foremost concerns. Their first homes where not the traditional log houses associated with the pioneer era -- those would be built later if the family managed to survive.

In 1876, the elderly James McCallum of Giles County, Tennessee, described conditions he remembered among people who had erected homesteads on the wrong side of the Indian boundary. It was rare, he said, to find a cabin in this wilderness with more than one room. Their floors were usually made from either packed clay or partially hewned logs that had been placed in mud with the flat side up. Roofs were fastened by wooden poles placed side by side, or by rough boards that were weighted at both ends. Leather strips served as hinges for the doors and windows. Buckskin curtains were sometimes strung up to provide a degree of privacy in the room.

McCallum wrote about the desperation of those squatters who had been forcibly removed from their homes by the federal soldiers stationed at Fort Hampton in 1810 and 1811; "On the Alabama side, the Reduses and Simmses and those who settled Simms' settlement were driven off and they went back over the line and built camps and shanties which they covered with bark...stripped from the trees like tan bark...I saw the camps...when I was a boy..."

Small patches of corn and gardens of vegetables and herbs could be seen around these wilderness cabins. There were fish from the rivers and streams as well as wild fruit and honey from the hills and hollows. Wild game was plentiful and an important part of the food supply. In his early history of Limestone County, Captain R. A. McClellan interviewed an elderly lady whom he called "Aunt Lila McKinney." She told about the time her husband, Alex, killed fifteen deer in one day. He strung their carcasses on tree limbs and ordered her to bring them home. Aunt Lila refused; allowing the meat "to rot in the trees."

Regardless of how they saw themselves these earliest settlers in what is now Lauderdale and Limestone Counties were squatters on Indian lands. Following the 1816 Treaty with the Chickasaw Nation, many of them remained in the area. A few of them managed to purchase their original homesteads, while others acquired parcels of land elsewhere. Many of them, no doubt, moved away and did not return. Yet, these were the first of the white pioneers to make their homes in the wilderness of the Muscle Shoals and Northwest Alabama.

THE LEGENDARY FIRST SETTLER OF FLORENCE

According to old legends, the first settler of Florence was John Johnson. Although there is no known proof to verify this story, there is an indenture, dated August 3, 1807, between John D. Chisholm and the State of Georgia, which shows that a Captain John Johnson was granted a lease of 1,000 acres of land for a period of 99 years and renewable for 900 years. This acreage was described as being a part of the Doublehead Reserve on the Tennessee River "at a place known as the Muscle Shoals." Doublehead's Reserve lay on the North side of the Tennessee River between Cypress Creek on the west and Elk River on the east.

There were old-timers in previous years who believed that Johnson's 1,000 acres were part of the large tract that was later surveyed as the Town of Florence.

Captain Johnson's name does not appear on any of the later petitions made in 1809 and 1810 which lists the tenants and intruders on Doublehead's Reserve. If, indeed, John Johnson did reside at the present site of Florence, he perhaps had returned to Tennessee by 1809. Prior to 1816, his daughter, Lucinda Johnson, was married to Major Lewis Dillahunty of Davidson County, Tennessee, and a hero in the War of 1812.

Early in 1816, Lewis and Lucinda Johnson Dillahunty, immigrated to North Alabama, and are credited as being, the founders of Courtland. Major Dillahunty had been appointed in some official capacity by President James Monroe. One source says he was involved with the surveying of former Indian lands.

In his book, *Early Settlers of Alabama* (1899), James Saunders wrote about Dillahunty's position: "Whether he was an Indian agent or a confidential emissary of the government, I have not been able to ascertain."

After three years, the Dillahuntys moved from Courtland to a place near Colbert County's historic Old Brick Presbyterian Church, North of Leighton. In 1825, they were in Hardeman County, Tennessee, where the major died in 1826. Historian James Saunders wrote that while the Dillahuntys lived near Leighton, the major purchased lands both for his father, Thomas Dillahunty, and for his father-in- law, John Johnson.

However, Colbert County land records show that John Johnson purchased eighty acres North of Leighton in 1829 for $600. Here he built a brick house, known today as "Green Onion," which is considered as one of the most historic structures in North Alabama. Of interest, also, is that the Lauderdale County Courthouse records show that in 1826, Henry Smith, a prominent planter, purchased a large tract of land, known then as the John Johnson Place, near the present Smithsonia community.

Perhaps there is no name in Scotland and in America more popular or more frequently used than the name John Johnson. Yet, it is interesting to speculate that an old myth may be correct: that John Johnson and his wife may have been the first settlers of Florence, and that a house they built in Colbert County stands today as a treasured relic of the past.

THE LEGACY OF GABE BUTLER

It would be difficult to find a more hardy pioneer than Gabriel Butler who arrived in Lauderdale County while the Indians were here. Gabriel, Thomas, John, and Richard Butler were listed as tenants on the Doublehead Reserve in 1809. Two years later they were forced to abandon their homes, crops, and fields by United States troops from nearby Fort Hampton. These soldiers had been sent here to keep white people out of Indian Territory.

This did not deter Gabriel Butler. Five years later, following a treaty with the Chickasaw Nation, he was back on Blue Water Creek between Center Star and Elgin. It was not until 1822, however, that by good management he became financially able to purchase the legal title to his farm.

Gabe was born in North Carolina about the time of the American Revolution. It was said that he had no particular destination in mind when he gathered his large family and began his trek across the mountains into what was known as the old Southwest. All his earthly possessions were on the back of a pack mule which he led with a rope while his wife and children trailed along behind.

Perhaps the family had reached Tennessee by the time Gabe heard Chief Doublehead had made arrangements through an agent, John Chisholm, to lease land to white tenants for a period of 99 years with a 900 year renewable clause. Most of East Lauderdale County, known as the "Doublehead Reserve," had been set aside for this wily old chief when the Cherokee Nation ceded this part of their territory in 1806. Doublehead was assassinated a year later by his own people.

The Butlers lived in a make-shift tent while their first log house was being constructed from the forest. Afterwards they moved into a more accommodating two-story structure known as the "high house" that was perched on a hill overlooking Blue Water Creek.

Gabe Butler was an Elder in the Baptist Church. It is believed that he was responsible for establishing the first meeting place for the Baptists in Lauderdale County. Its original location was noted by Reverend Wesley Smith who later became a Methodist circuit rider: "In the Blue Water bottom near Squire McDougal's was a beautiful beech grove, under the branches of which the Baptists had erected a stand for preaching." This is believed to have been the forerunner of the Blue Water Creek Baptist Church which was established in 1823 with eleven charter members. One of the Butler descendants wrote that Gabriel Butler "... built the Bluewater Primitive Baptist Church house on his own land and at his own expense. After some time the congregation moved across Blue Water and built another place of worship."

Following a long and fruitful life, Gabriel died just prior to the Civil War. His descendants in Lauderdale County are almost innumerable. There is a large engraved stone on the west bank of Blue Water Creek that marks the approximate location of his grave. It is in a cemetery that was once a part of his pioneer farm. Gabriel Butler was one of the unsung heroes of the frontier. His monument serves as a reminder of the tough fiber and dogged determination found among the original settlers who, lived in a wilderness that would one day become the Muscle Shoals.

THE PIONEERS WHO CAME TO STAY

Folklore sometimes provides glimpses into the past. A fleeting look into how life was in the wilderness can be found in the tales that have been handed down by the descendants of John David and Catherine Stutts Richardson. This brave, persistent, and hardy family settled on Blue Water

Creek between Green Hill and Lexington when this was Indian country. They were among Lauderdale county's first families.

Catherine Stutts Richardson Born 1777 – Died 1876, Wife of John David Richardson. A noble heroin of The Muscle Shoals wilderness.

Old records of Moore County, North Carolina, show that around 1808 a caravan of forty-two families left that area in search of new lands beyond the mountains in the newly opened Mississippi Territory. Most of these people, includeing the McDougal's, McDonalds, Kennedy's, Keys, Muse's, Fry's, and Dannelly's, waited in Tennessee until after the 1816 Treaty with the Chickasaw Nation to acquire land in what was to become Lauderdale County, Alabama.

The Richardson's, who were among this large caravan, continued their trek. According to folktale, they were trying to find the Natchez Trace which hopefully would guide them into the Mississippi country. By chance, however, they took a wrong path and entered what is now North Alabama by way of the Old Doublehead Trace. This Indian road ran from Franklin, Tennessee to Doublehead's Village near the mouth of Blue Water Creek in East Lauderdale County.

140

They soon became aware that they were lost in what appeared to be a foreboding place. Upon arriving at Blue Water Creek they found bluffs too steep for their wagons to cross. While waiting for the men to cut a bypass around the cliffs they discovered friendly Indians, bountiful game in the forest, and plenty of cane alongside the creek to feed their horses and cattle. Thus, the Richardson's began to build their cabin on land that is known to this day as the Old Richardson Place.

They were not here long until they were found by federal soldiers from Fort Hampton and forced to move across the line into Giles County, Tennessee. There are a number of family legends which describe the circumstances of this family crisis. One tale is that a child was too sick to be moved and the soldiers gave the family permission to stay until it recovered. By nightfall this child was buried near the cabin and by daylight the family was on their way into Tennessee.

The Richardson's were soon back on the same land, and some say in the same cabin. John David Richardson became one of the first land buyers at the federal land sale in 1818. He purchased two tracts around his cabin that year and a third tract the following year. He died prior to the Civil War. His widow, Catherine, was about a hundred years old at the time of her death in 1876. Known as "Granny Kate", she became a legend. There are numerous stories about her life and especially about her encounters with Yankee soldiers during the Civil War.

A cemetery near Center Hill bears her name today, and local residents sometimes refer to the section of Blue Water Creek that flows through the old Richardson farm as "Granny's Creek."

The Richardson's are about as ingrained in the early history of Lauderdale County as the limestone that lies under its hills and hollows. They were blessed with a stamina that enabled them to survive even when they had become lost in the wilderness.

CAMPBELL'S FERRY

Near the beginning of the 19th century, a man by the name of Campbell established a ferry near the present Wilson Dam. It is believed that he was the Captain Campbell who was reported to be "building houses and making improvements at Doublehead's" in 1804. This captain had earlier been in charge of a garrison along the Tennessee River.

Census reports reveal at least five Campbells living in the Mississippi Territory in 1809: William, Robert, Gustavus, Peter, and Alexander. Militia appointments in the Southwest Territory, dated as early as 1787, show three Campbells John, Robert, and Solomon who were commissioned as either a lieutenant or captain.

It is interesting that Major Butler, who began the first survey for the proposed Jackson Military Road in 1817, evidently intended to use Campbells Ferry for its river crossing. However, because of illness, he was replaced by another surveyor, H. Young. In his report to General Andrew Jackson, written from Shoal Creek on September 30, 1817, Young stated that Major Butler "commenced the line at Campbell's Ferry and continued for 86 miles."

Young ran his line to the mouth of Cypress Creek. It is conjectured that either Jackson or General John Coffee may have had a hand in this decision. By then both men had visited this area and were impressed with a high plateau above the river which a year later would be laid out as the town of Florence.

A typical pioneer log house.
(The Kennedy Home, in Cowpen Creek near Green Hill.)

What better promotion for a frontier town than to have a national highway running through the middle of it!

THE LEGEND OF ANDREW JACKSON & CRAIG'S INN

Craig's Inn may be Lauderdale County's oldest existing pioneer structure. Some think it could have been built as early as 1810. Its hewn logs are now concealed beneath the modern home of Eula and William Hunt who live almost directly behind the cemetery at Lone Cedar Church of Christ on the old Jackson Highway.

Samuel Craig established an inn and Indian trading post at this intersection of two aboriginal roads in about 1810. One path ran from Buffalo River, ten miles North of Lawrenceburg, Tennessee, to the mouth of Cypress Creek below Florence where it

143

lined with other trails South of the river. This road was used by Andrew Jackson during the War of 1812. Old Hickory was so pleased by this short-cut, he later had it improved to become the Jackson Military Road.

The east-to-west trail that passed near the inn connected Ditto's Landing below Huntsville with Savannah, Tennessee. It crossed Shoal Creek at Savannah Ford near the Tennessee Line. Sections of this abandoned road can be seen today by following County Roads 63, 64, 34, and 37.

Craig was born about 1785 in orange County, North Carolina. His father was probably the Irish immigrant, John Craig. Two brothers, John and Andrew Craig, were veterans of the American Revolution. Samuel Craig was in Maury County, Tennessee, as early as 1808. On December 17, 1810, four Craig brothers Samuel, John, Johnston and David divided 3,200 acres of Maury County land that had been granted to their father for his service in the Revolution. Three of these brothers Samuel, David, and John were early and buyers at Florence.

Samuel Craig was among the 108 petitioners in 1810 requesting that they be allowed to remain in Chief Doublehead's Reserve in Lauderdale Court. He came here following his marriage to a Miss Gordon in Maury County Tennessee, that same year. Chickasaw Chief George Colbert, ferryman on the nearby Natchez Trace, had complained to the federal government about these "white intruders." As a result, soldiers were sent to move these people back into Tennessee. Having been forced out of Alabama, Craig then moved to Grinders Stand, Tennessee, there he established another inn and dry goods storage the Natchez Trace. About 1813 however, he was back at his inn in Lauderdale County. Eleven small one room log cottages each, with a fireplace, were built

144

on the grounds to accommodate travelers who were now arriving by stage coach, wagons and horseback. Craig advertised that his rooms were individually heated.

One of the vagaries of local history is the military presence of Andrew Jackson at the Muscle Shoals during the War of 1812. Historians agree he was there, but dates have never been pinpointed. Early James Jackson family papers locate a field North of St. Florian, near the intersection of Bailey Springs Road and the Old Jackson Highway, as the site where the Tennessee Volunteers camped on their way home from New Orleans 1815. Also, Amus Wilks talked of watching Jackson and his soldiers as they passed his blacksmith shop and store near Florence. Old legends tell how General Jackson, after camping his men, crossed Shoal Creek in his carriage with Rachael and little Andrew to spend the night at Craig's Inn. It has been said that this was the beginning of the friendship between Old Hickory and Samuel Craig. Earl newspapers show when Andrew Jackson was entertained at Florence in 1826, one of his friends who hosted the dinner was the innkeeper, Samuel Craig.

Faded records do not tell what happened to Craig and his inn. It is known that his wife was sickly. In 1829, she was living at Bailey Springs, two years before Jonathan Bailey opened his health resort. However, Bailey later used her "testimony" to advertise the "healing powers" of his mineral springs. Old newspaper announcements indicate the inn had been leased in 1825 to two men named Turner and Sessums. Courthouse records show Samuel Craig purchased 80 acres near Goose Shoals on Shoal Creek in 1827 and another 75 acres west of Shoal Creek in 1830. John Watkins acquired Craig's Inn in the late 1840's. His son Charlie Watkins, who was born in 1857, told of the eleven cabins and always referred to his father's farm as the old Craig place.

Craig's old inn was also a Civil War site. On November 6, 1864, Colonel Datus E. Coon camped there with his cavalry brigade, consisting of the Sixth Illinois, the Ninth Illinois, the Second Iowa, along with, Company K, First Illinois Light Artillery. They remained about nine days as they guarded the ford at Shoal Creek and watched the activities of Confederate General John Bell Hood at Florence. Coon reported a number of enemy activities in and around the ford as well as at other locations while his men were at what was then, the Watkins farm.

Few places in Lauderdale County have been involved in more history than this farm on Bretherick Creek known as old Craig's Inn. In a span of some fifty years, it was a trading post for passing Indians, a legendary resting place for the Hero of New Orleans, and as a cavalry camp for an invading colonel of the Union Army.

LIFE IN THE MUSCLE SHOALS WILDERNESS

In the Summer of 1802, Silas Dinsmoor, the newly appointed Chocktaw Indian Agent was surprised to find a white woman at the Muscle Shoals. Dinsmoor, who had earlier served as an agent for the Cherokees, was traveling to his new post over the Natchez Trace. On this trip he stopped long enough to help settle a dispute among the Chickasaws and a number of Delaware Indians who were then living on Chickasaw lands.

Dinsmoor described this woman as being a daughter of a man by the name of Adams "who has resided some time among the Cherokees with part of his family, a pretty dismal group lazy and shiftless." These people were squatters on Indian lands.

146

Attempts had been made in 1785 and again in 1791 to establish settlements at the Shoals. Each time, however, they were thwarted by the Indians or by the federal government. Yet, there is evidence, as suggested by Dinsmoor's memorandum, that people began drifting into this part of the wilderness around the turn of the nineteenth century. Most of them, perhaps, came by way of the Natchez Trace.

A document, dated March 15, 1804, referred to a Captain Campbell, commander of a garrison, who was building houses and making large improvements within three miles of Cherokee Chief Doublehead's village near the mouth of Blue Water Creek. There was a crossing of the river known as Campbell's Ferry just above the present site of Wilson Dam.

A white intruder named Arnold died in 1806. He left behind four horses, two saddles and bridles, one gold watch, a fowling piece, one rifle, and a trunk containing sugar, tea, and other condiments. This was an impressive list of belongings for one who had been living among the Indians.

A report by the Secretary of War, dated April 2, 1806, shows that more than twenty families were at the Shoals. These, he said, were in addition to Moses Melton who was at Melton's Bluff near the head of the Muscle Shoals in present day Lawrence County.

It was not until the 1818 Huntsville Land Sales, almost a year before Alabama was admitted as the twenty-second state, that land in this part of the state could be legally acquired. It was as if a flood-gate had been opened. People from Tennessee, Georgia, Kentucky, Virginia, the Carolinas, and other places rushed in to become its settlers. It had been a slow, yet steady transition from that day when Silas Dinsmoor by chance ran into a white woman at the Muscle Shoals.

FLORENCE'S FIRST BUSINESSMAN

Amos Wilkes was a grocer and a blacksmith. His combination store and blacksmith shop was at the intersection of two early Indian trails as early as 1810. Ruins of an abandoned well near St. Bartholomew's Episcopal Church mark the site of this first commercial adventure at Florence.

This served, principally, as a trading post for the Indians. These two roads that intersected in front of Wilkes' store and shop connected with a number of Indian villages on the North bank, of the Tennessee. One of these trails led to the mouth of Cypress Creek, which served as a crossing point toward other Indian communities South of the Tennessee River.

The name "Amus Wilkes" is listed as one of the 107 white settlers in Meigs District at the Muscle Shoals. Meigs, of course, was Colonel Return Jonathan Meigs, the Cherokee Indian Agent, who at the time was trying to remove the settlers from Indian lands through military action.

Although Wilkes and his family were among those who were evicted in the Spring of 1811, they were back at the same location as early as 1815. This was the year that the Army of Andrew Jackson, after the Battle of New Orleans, followed a series of Indian paths to discover a short cut on their way home to Nashville.

Many years after Jackson's march through what would become Florence, Wilkes remembered that the soldiers passed in front of his house and store. The army camped for the night near the

Bailey Springs Road a few miles west of Shoal Creek. This military route that shortened the distance between Nashville and New Orleans was improved during the years 1817 to 1820 to become the Jackson Military Road.

In the early part of the Twentieth Century it became U.S. Highway 43. A number of the people who had built homes and cleared land on Doublehead's Reserve prior to 1811, were fortunate enough to acquire legal titles to the same property following the 1816 Treaty with the Indians. This was not the case, however, for Amos Wilkes and his wife, Elizabeth. Instead of returning to their former homestead, they purchased a farm on Little Cypress Creek. The Wilkes probably had too much competition in that, their earlier site and surrounding tracts were purchased by a number of land speculators, including Waddy Tate, John Brahan, William and Thomas McDonald, and the Cypress Land Company.

Amos Wilkes' first tract of land was entered March 7,1818, and the second on April 7 of the same year. Both tracts totaled 240 acres. The 1830 Census lists five slaves in the Wilkes household.

Amos Wilkes, who was born in 1770, died sometime after 1844. He and his wife, Elizabeth, who was ten years younger than Amos, are probably buried in unmarked graves somewhere near their Middle Cypress Creek farm. They were the forerunners of all the merchants who have been a part of the economic life of the City of Florence.

A PIONEER LADY WHO SAVED HER HOME

The story of Polly Allen and how she outwitted a contingent of soldiers to save her home and possessions is one of the most interesting chapters to come out of the early frontier life in Lauderdale County.

Polly was the first wife of Captain Henry D. Allen, believed to have been one of Andrew Jackson's soldiers of the Indian Wars and the Battle of New Orleans.

The Allen's were among the first to buy land in Lauderdale County in 1818, following the Indian treaties that, in effect, opened up the area for settlement. However, they had previously lived in Lauderdale County as early as 1811, but were among those who were driven out of the Indian lands and back across the line into Tennessee.

Polly Allen's heroism is a part of the story of the very earliest white settlement in Lauderdale County. It occurred in the Spring of 1811 at Blue Water Creek near what would someday become the town of Lexington.

A number of families moved into the Indian Territory between Elk River and Cypress Creek in the early 1800's, before there was a county or state.

These pioneers were brave and hardy souls. Much has been written about their hardships and how they survived, but little has been said about the women of those pioneer homes who braved the elements, extremely primitive living conditions, and constant threats from hostile Indians.

Mary Barnes "Polly" Allen was born in Edgecombe County of North Carolina. Her father, Joseph Barnes, was a veteran of the Revolutionary War. She married Henry Allen at Sumner County, Tennessee, where she had moved with her parents from North Carolina.

Captain Henry Davis Allen was born March 26, 1782, also in Edgecombe County, North Carolina, and had migrated, likewise, with his parents to Sumner County, Tennessee. Henry's father, Rhody Allen, born in 1742, was a Methodist Circuit Rider, and a native of Maryland. In 1804, Henry and Polly, moved with his parents to Maury County, Tennessee.

While living in Maury County they heard stories about the Muscle Shoals, known then as "Mussel Shoals". Prior to 1811, the Allen's, including Henry, Polly, and their young children, along with Henry's father, crossed over the Tennessee State line into Indian Territory. One of Henry's sisters and her husband, William Maxey, and children, were a part of this small caravan who settled along Blue Water Creek.

There were a number of white settlers in the area. Some had arrived prior to the Allens, and some came afterwards. A number of these people possessed what was known as "Tomahawk Claims". These were land leases granted by the Indians that recognized their right to occupy Indian lands.

However, the Allens, along with a number of others, were squatters. They had no deed, no claim, and, according to the complaints of the Indians, had no right to be in the area.

The Allens lived part of their first winter in the wilderness in a tent that had been part of their cargo in their move from Tennessee. This was soon replaced, however, by a temporary shelter Henry and his father made from poles and bark. Meanwhile, a log house was being constructed a short distance from this make-shift arrangement.

They managed to clear some land in time to plant a small crop by early spring that first year. More land had been cleared for cultivation by the following spring, and by 1811, the Allens had a barn and other outbuildings on their small farm in the Indian country. Although things had improved somewhat for the Allens, the primitive conditions in the wilderness were still harsh and severe. Family stories that have been handed down, tell of, wolves eating bread at the back door of their small dwelling in the forest.

In the early spring of 1811, after weeks of heavy rains and the subsequent flooding of the creeks and rivers, the soldiers came. Their mission was to destroy the homes and crops of the squatter's on Indian land and to force them back across the Tennessee State line. They reached the Allen cabin in three days following their dispatch from Fort Hampton near Elk River. They had burned a number of other houses along the way.

Henry D. Allen was away from home when they arrived. Polly gathered her small family at the front door to face the troops, as a number of them had dismounted and were standing in the front yard. The officer in charge read an order signed by the Cherokee Indian Agent, Colonel Return J. Meigs, that, proclaimed the soldiers had been sent to burn their house and to order them out of the territory.

Then, this pioneer heroine of early Lauderdale County did something the soldiers had not expected. She offered to prepare them a meal before they burned her home. Obviously, the soldiers were hungry. Their rations for three days had consisted only of dried venison, called "jerky" and dried corn, known as "hardtack".

The soldiers milled around the place while Polly Allen cooked what food she had. Soon, they were served a bountiful meal, and the cavalrymen lined up to take their turn filling their plates.

Then came the hard part: The soldiers, after being treated so graciously by Polly Allen, set fire to the cabin and rode away. But this was not the end of the story. Two of the soldiers, as has been recorded, fell behind the others. They returned and extinguished the flames. Polly Allen's quick thinking and kindness had saved her home and possessions.

The Allen family, however, were soon driven from the Indian country. It was during this period of his life Henry D. Allen is believed to have joined the Tennessee Volunteers with Andrew Jackson to fight the Indians, and, later, to fight in the Battle of New Orleans against the British. Allen was made a Captain, and was with Jackson as the army returned from New Orleans along a route that passed near the place on Blue Water Creek where earlier he had made his home.

Polly Allen and Captain Henry D. Allen, along with their children, returned to the Blue Water Creek site following the treaties with the Indians that opened up the country for settlement. On March 4, 1818, he entered 80 acres of land. Allen's rank entitled him to a considerable amount of land, and through the years he entered hundreds of acres in East Lauderdale County. The Allen Cemetery and Allen Park at Blue Water Creek are located on the site of the early home of Henry D. Allen and his wife, Polly.

Following Polly Allen's death in 1856, Henry married Mary Robertson, a widow considerably younger than this veteran of the Indian Campaigns and the War of 1812.

Captain Henry Davis Allen died May 25, 1873 at the age of 91 years. There are numbers of families in Lauderdale County who can trace their heritage to these courageous people who came early and made their home alongside Blue Water Creek, and among the hostile Indians who insisted they be removed from their land.

TIMES AND EVENTS AT HERMAN SPRINGS

There are many historic sites and places in North Alabama. It would be hard to locate one more meaningful to the earliest beginnings than Herman Springs. Through the years, however, the pronunciation has been changed to "Harmon Springs". Herman, or "Harmon" Springs is located in an isolated and almost forgotten Herman, or "Harmon" Hollow, a few miles Southeast of Center Star, near the mouth of Blue Water Creek, in East Lauderdale County.

Early Indians, it is said, found "healing spirits" among these waters. Old timers claimed that this spring was purer and colder than, all the other water heads in the area.

This bold natural spring, fed by several streams, was a part of the early Phillips plantation. However, before the Civil War, Phillips sold his land to Benjamin Taylor, and during the reconstruction period moved to Lexington to establish a business. Taylor's daughter, Susan Polk Taylor, married Captain Jonathan McDavid Cunningham, and for the next 100 years this 3,600-acre estate was operated by his descendants, and was known as the Cunningham Plantation. Even in more recent years, until it sold in 1964, it had an ante-bellum "big house", plantation store, grist mill, blacksmith shop, and close to thirty individual homes for the farm workers. The big house burned in the early 1980's.

Captain Cunningham made a name for himself as a Confederate Officer during the Civil War. Later, he demonstrated the same leadership capabilities as a State Senator in Montgo-

154

mery. During the last years of his long and eventful life, the Captain was confined to bed. According to his body servant, Will Bulls, the "Old Boss" would frequently request that Will go all the way to Herman Springs to "fetch" a bucket of water, even, though there was plenty of good, cold water closer to the house.

But long before the time of the Phillips, Taylors and Cunning-hams, Herman Springs played a role in the very earliest settlements of Northwest Alabama. More importantly, it is belie-ved that the first white child born in what was to become Laud-erdale County, occurred in Herman Hollow at Herman Springs about the year 1810.

Israel Herman came from Tennessee about 1807 and built a small one-room log cabin in this hollow and alongside this spring. His nearest neighbors were Indians who lived in Chief Doublehead's village on the other side of Blue Water Creek. However, there were other white settlers in the area who began arriving around 1807. Many of these people were on good terms with the Indians and, in fact, had leases signed by Cherokee Chief Doublehead for a period of 99 years. Most of these homesteads were located in the area between Elk River and Cypress Creek.

There were others who were called "squatters". These were the intruders on Indian lands who did not hold either leases or "tomahawk claims". The Cherokees objected and asked the Federal Government to remove them from the territory. How-ever, the most vocal opposition to their presence was Chief George Colbert of the Chickasaw Nation.

They were asked to move back across the Tennessee state line. In fact, to insure their removal, the U.S. Government sent troops into the area. This company of soldiers, under Captain Alexander Smythe, built Fort Hampton on Elk River. Their mission was to remove the white people from the Indian lands and, also, to prevent others from coming in. These people tried desperately to remain at their new homes, and even petitioned the President of the United States for relief from the expulsion order.

In a speech delivered on July 4, 1876 at Florence, Judge William Basil Wood made the following remarks:

> "William Herman, Esquire, who lives in the neighborhood of Center Star, was born in this county in the year 1810, and he is the oldest native born citizen of the county now living, perhaps the first white child born in the county."

Sometime after 1876, William Herman moved to Texas. The Florence Gazette published a letter from him in the April 19, 1884 edition. This is his story, in part:

> "...born under the sound of the Mussel Shoals of Tennessee River, March 11th, 1810, the first white child born in the County, so said. My parents had settled near the river in that territory, though without authority. ...The county was wild, full of trials and hardship, uncultivated and but little civilization...so many white settlers came in that the Indians complained to the Government, and we were burned out of house and home and driven to Tennessee."

The soldiers from Fort Hampton made a number of raids. Their orders were to burn everything the settler owned to insure that there would be no means of survival in the Indian Territory.

They found the Herman cabin in the early Spring of 1811. There had been days and weeks of hard rains, and Blue Water Creek was out of its banks. Yet, the soldiers and their horses swam the strong current to lay waste everything that Israel Herman and his family had built: their home, the barn, out-buildings and even the fences that had been erected where their crops were to be planted. But cruel treatment and hard times were not new to these people. Will Herman's letter continues:

> "My father and mother had lived through the Colonial Revolution, brought up under the traditions of witchcraft, their minds full of all the horrors of the revolution and the massacres of the Indians."

The Federal Government, under the supervision of Colonel Return J. Meigs, the Cherokee Indian Agent, managed to drive out the white settlers from the land that would someday become Lauderdale County. But, most of them came back. The Hermans, following the Indian Treaties, moved back to their Herman Hollow and rebuilt their home alongside Herman Springs. Herman's 1884 letter tells of their return:

> "...my father returned to his old settlement where I was reared, barefoot, and in buck-skin trousers and hunting shirt, farming, fishing, hunting and trapping for a livelihood."

Will Herman's recollections of those pioneer days weave an interesting fabric into the history of the early settlers in North Alabama. Nothing was wasted and every means had to be used to survive. In one of his stories he relates how he and his brother caught a deer without guns or ammunition. This chase happened on one of the coldest days of the year, occurring in the Tennessee River near the mouth of Blue Water Creek. The two brothers were in a canoe at what was known as the deer crossing. Once the deer was in the water there was no need for ammunition, which was always in short supply on the fron-tier.

Their waiting paid off as soon a large buck appeared and began its swim for the other shore. The Herman boys caught the deer about mid-way in the river. As was their plan, Will grabbed the deer by its tail while his brother clubbed it to death with the oar. According to Herman's story, however, the water was so cold that his hands grew numb and he almost lost his prey. He resolved the situation, though, by clutching the large deer with his teeth, managing to hold on until they both were able to pull the buck into the canoe.

Long before the white man came, Center Star, was the site, at different times, of at least two Indian villages. It became one of the first white settlements in Lauderdale County, mainly because of its fertile lands, some of which had already been cleared by the Indians.

The first Methodist congregation in Lauderdale County was established at this site, and when the first Methodist circuit riders arrived in June 1818, there was already a Baptist brush arbor meeting place in existence near the mouth of Blue Water Creek. And according to what sketchy records are available, it could have been at Herman Springs near Center Star where Lauderdale County's first white child was born.

Although this claim has been made, there is a record of the birth of Mary Richardson in the area of Lexington, Alabama on May 30, 1800. This could have occurred either in what later was to become Lauderdale County, or possibly across the Tennessee state line within the vicinity of Lexington. She was known as Aunt Polly Gresham, the wife of Thomas Gresham, and was 98 years of age at the time of her death, April 10, 1898.

10 Inventories Of White Families Prior to 1812

A pioneer lady believed to have lived near Green Hill in Lauderdale County, Alabama (Courtesy of L. D. Staggs, Jr.).

THE EARLIEST SETTLERS ON INDIANS LANDS

The Cherokee relinquished their claims to what is now Lauderdale and Limestone Counties, except a large tract of between Cypress Creek and Elk River which became known as Doublehead Reserve. However, the Chickasaw maintained that they held title to the land North of the Tennessee River in Northwest Alabama all the way to the line between what is now

Limestone County and Madison County. White settlers began arriving in this area in relatively large numbers soon after the beginning of the 19th century. By mid 1810 it was estimated 2,250 white people were in this part of the Chickasaw land, in addition to the number who were in Doublehead's Reserve, either with or without permission.

The Indian land South of the Tennessee State line and North of the Tennessee River, and especially at the Muscle Shoals, became a serious problem following the Treaty of Tellico in 1798. The white man, according to the Cherokees, "traveled faster than Indian treaties", and were encroaching in relatively large numbers on the territory known as Doublehead's Reserve between Elk River and Cypress Creek as early as 1807.

Although Chief Doublehead was a Cherokee, he was, according to his son-in-law Chief George Colbert of the Chickasaw Nation, occupying their land by permission. Doublehead through his agent, John Chisholm, leased thousands of acres of land in this reserve for 99 years, with a 900-year renewable clause.

Both Cherokees and Chickasaws were unhappy about these leases, as well as the presence of squatters, who had no claim or right to the land they were clearing and occupying. This grievance, it is believed, was the principal cause of Doublehead's assassination by his own tribesmen in 1807. The Chickasaws, prodded by Colbert, petitioned the Federal Government time and again to remove the white people from their lands.

Cherokee Indian Agent, Colonel Return J. Meigs, was ordered by the U. S. Government to remove the settlers from the territory. His first command post for this purpose was established as Fort Collins, named for Colonel Robert Collins in East Tennessee. On June 12, 1809 Meigs wrote the Acting Secretary of War that he had removed 201 families from the Chickasaw lands in what would become North Alabama. According to this report, his soldiers marched over 400 miles in a campaign that took 51 days.

A year later, however; the white intruders were back on the land, a large number of them occupying their original home sites. This brought about so much pressure from the Chickasaws that the Federal Government ordered General Wade Hampton to establish a fort near the Muscle Shoals.

Fort Hampton was built, probably in 1810, about four miles from the mouth of Elk River near the western boundary of Limestone County. It was an unusual army fort in Indian country, in that there were no stockade walls enclosing it. The post was mainly a cantonment consisting of a field office and twenty-four cabins for housing the soldiers. Captain Alexander Symthe was the first commanding officer. Sometime later he was replaced by Captain George Washington Sevier, the son of the old Indian fighter and first Governor of Tennessee, John Sevier.

Colonel Meigs was dispatched to Fort Hampton to personally oversee the task of again removing the white settlers, as well as building a series of roads running from the fort to other strategic areas. Before these settlers could be forced to leave, it was necessary for Colonel Meigs to determine who they were and where they lived. Thus, a number of documents were prepared for Meigs. In addition, at least one petition was created by the settlers who were appealing to the President of the United States for permission to remain in the Indian country.

These papers make up a fairly accurate census of the people who made their home in what was to become Lauderdale County and the Northeastern section of Limestone County some ten or eleven years prior to the creation of these two counties. A few of these early families gave their names to creeks, springs, villages and other features in the area.

1807 LIST OF LEASE HOLDERS ON DOUBLEHEAD'S RESERVE

(Cherokee Receipt Book and Journal, War Department 1801-1809, Colonel Meigs, Number 67, pages 91-96.)

Andrew Baxter	Thomas Heard
Stephen Gatlin	Zac'y Phillips
Henry Lucas	Ezek'l E. Park
Oliver Porter	Zac'y Sims
Wm. Randal	Tyre Dabney
John Coffee	Adam Hunter
Wm. Harris	Sam'l Hemphill
Wm. Watson	Joseph Phillips
John Lucas, Jr.	John Towers
Willis Randal	Isham S. Fannin
Cuthburt Collier	Jacobs Mitchell
Thomas Ligon	Barlet Towns
Abraham Heard	Rob't Sims
Rob't Lucas	Thomas Cooper
Peter Robinson	John T. Colquet
Dan'l Flournay	George Heard

"Indenture made 3 Day of August 1807 between John D. Chisholm in behalf of himself and attorney in fact for Doublehead an Indian Chief in the Cherokee Nation of the one part and of the State of Georgia, of the other part: lease formed to the aforesaid lessees: tract or parcel of land on the North side of the Tennessee River at a place known as the Muscle Shoals, bounded Southwardly by the Tennessee River west-wardly by a creek called Tee-Kee-ta-no-eh (Cypress) east-wardly by Chee-wa-lee (Elk River) and from a point ten miles North on Elk River to same on Cypress Creek except the fol-lowing reservations on said tract:

Hudson Alford	800 acres
Capt. John Hays	6,000 acres
Wm. Burney	12,000 acres
Wm. Hester	100 acres
Thomas Butler	1,200 acres
Dr. McPherson	12,000 acres
John D. Chisholm	1,000 acres
Lodwick Moore	600 acres
John Crogmiles	640 acres
P. McPherson	64,000 acres
John Crudep	480 acres
Fred Peeler	12,000 acres
Doublehead	1,500 acres
Widow Smith & bro	2,560 acres
Calwell Estridge	200 acres
Wm. Stephens	100 acres
Capt John Johnson	1,000 acres
To Town & Ferry	640 acres
Total:	53,460 acres

To the above company a 99 year lease -Renewable for 900 years - consideration to be paid in four installments."

1809 LIST OF TENANTS ON DOUBLEHEAD RESERVE

A Man Name Unknown

Thomas Hull

Wm. Weir

Hudson Alford

Moses Jones

Mr. Hemphill

Julius Alford

David Keeler

Finey Thomas

Sam Anderson

John Keeler

Thomas Hays

Mr. Birdwell

Wm. Burner

Gabriel Butler

Mr. Kooley

James Taylor

John Butler

Adam Lackey

John Hays

Richard Butler

Mr. Longane

Harmon Hays

Thomas Butler

James Milstead

Benj'm Rays

Clark: & Hall

Zellous Milstead

Dr. Porter

James Cummings

Benj'm Moore

Mr. Hatch

Cullin Earp

Dr. McPherson

Fred' k Peeler

Josiah Glover

Mr. Keeler

Mr. Keeler Orig.

James Taylor

Names Unknown

1809 LIST OF WHITE INTRUDERS ON SHOAL CREEK & ELK RIVER

Intruders on Shoal Creek May 23-24, 1809:

Intruders on Shoal Creek 1809: Shoal Creek extended from the Tennessee River in Lauderdale County, Alabama, into Lawrence County, Tennessee. Therefore, these intruders were from both counties. The first name listed is Daniel Beeler who lived near present-day Lawrenceburg, Tennessee. The Beeler Fork of Shoal Creek was named for him.

Name:	Location:	Name:	Location:
James Coe	SW Branch	Sterling Clack	SW Branch
Daniel Beeler	East Branch	Wm. McFenal	E Branch
Jno Welch	E Fork	Jas. Tade	W Shoal
Wm. Hinson	W Shoal Cr	Jno. Chambers	E Branch
Wm. Shoate	W Fork	Sam Inman	W Fork
Jno. Shoate	W Fork	Wm. McCann	W Fork
Simon Higgs	E Branch	Geo. Circle	E Branch
Jno. Higgs	E Branch	Wm. McConnel	W Fork
Mays (2 in fam)	SW Br.	Alex Mackey	E Branch
Fred Shalley	W Shoal Cr	John Crawley	SW Branch
Ezek'l Heraldson	E Fork	Moses Crout	W Fork
Thos. Robinson	W Fork	Mr. Ben Cutbeard	W Fork
Richard Haley	SW Branch	Joel Phillips	W Shoal Cr
Spires Roach	SW Branch	John Haley	SW Branch
Mr. Hugh Randolph	E Branch		

Intruders on West Bank of Elk River, May 1809:

Name:	Location:	Name:	Location:
Andrew Coffen	W Bank	Mr. Freeman	W Bank
Mr. Peaton	W Bank	James Radish	W Bank
Geo. Harper	W Bank	Jno. Manasce	W Bank
Reuben Riggs	W Bank	Jno. Payne	W Bank
Jno. Reynolds	W Bank		

1810 LIST OF WHITE SETTLERS IN LAUDERDALE COUNTY

Ely Townsen Sr.	Matthew Jones	Amus Wilks
John Townsen	Hampton Strowell	Philop Mebery
Benjamin Birk	William Strowell	Frederick Peeler
James Cummins	Samuel Craig	Benjamin Yardley
David Hudspeth	Samuel Burney Sr.	Allen Kilough

W. W. Burney	Samuel Burney Jr.	Hennery Morehead
C. L. Burney	Charles L. Burney	Richard Haley
John Beard	John W. Burney	William Welch Jr.
John Butler	Hays	Rebekeah Hays
Gabriel Butler	Carlis Hays	Charles Moorehead
J. G. Hemphill	Georg Hays	William Welch
David Bains	Elisha Wilborn	Jeremiah Jos Lemaster
Benjamin Moore	Elisha Wilson	Willis Stevens
R. H. Alpes	James Hannegan	Thomas Yardley
Julius Alford	Jesse Stevens	Jonathan Little
Israel Harmon	James Young	Henry Tucker
Jno Crowly	Hutson Alford	Alexander Campbel
William Wilborn	Thomas Bowman	Jos C. Wilborn
Justin Readford	Matthew English	Andrew I. Kavanaugh
James Brion	Mosser Moss	Thos G. Butler
Adam Lacky	Benjamin Oberly	James Brown
James Hoopper	James Ellis	Jos Brown
M. Armstrong	Thos Reddish	James M. Petigrew
John Petigrew	Thomas Grisham	Richd Butler
Thomas Caplin	John Kilough	Edmund Hatch
D. B. Potter	David Kilough	James Welch
Joshua Golner	J. N. Coe	Thomas Casey
Nathaniel Casey	John Manley	Archabald Sanders
Joseph Edwards	Hennery Tucker	Benjamin Overby
John I. Moss	John Cavenner	Marlin Towns
Tyre G. Dabney	Joel Willbourn	James Wilbourn
William Wilbourn	Calton Wilborn	H. A. Hays
William Carwood	John Young	John Cole
Mason Moss	Abraham Cole Jr.	Abraham Cole Sr.
Alexander Carrel	Charles Hulsy	James Ellis
Moses Norman	Green Hudspeth	

(These people signed a petition to the President of the United States against removal from lands of Doublehead Reserve, circa 1810.)

Samuel Burney, Sr. soldier of the American Revolution, settled near present-day Rogersville.

THE EARLY HISTORY OF LAUDERDALE COUNTY

Lauderdale County was one of eight county governments created February 6, 1818, by the legislature of the Territory of Alabama, which makes it almost a year older than the State of Alabama. Previously what is now Lauderdale and Limestone Counties had been Elk County, which was created May 9, 1817, and dissolved January 26, 1818. Even earlier, what is now Lauderdale County had been a part of Houstoun County which was established in 1785 by the Georgia legislature. However, by 1804 Georgia had relinquished her claims to this part of the wilderness and Houstoun County ceased to exist. Lauderdale County was named for Lieutenant Colonel James Lauderdale who died December 23, 1814, from wounds received in the Battle of Talladega. He was one of five brothers who fought as officers under Andrew Jackson in the War of 1812.

Archaeological evidence shows that the first people to arrive at the Muscle Shoals occurred during the late stages of the Ice Age. These prehistoric nomads found bountiful food supplies here, including the small fresh water shellfish in the river and its tributaries. These mussels could be scooped up and eaten the year around.

When the first white adventurers and settlers arrived they found both the Chickasaw and Cherokee peoples at the Shoals. At one time their boundary lines overlapped about where Center Star is today. The Cherokee signed away their claims in 1806, but it was not until 1816 that the Chickasaw finally gave up this part of their ancient grounds.

There were a number of attempts to establish colonies here during the 1780's. These failed because of the hostilities of the local Native Americans. However, this was prime country much coveted by the white settlers. A report to the Secretary of War shows that more than twenty white families were living at the Shoals in 1806. When the Cherokee people ceded their land that year, they nevertheless held on to two reserves. One of these overlapped into Limestone County. The other included land from Elk River to Cypress Creek. Chief Doublehead began leasing land on these Doublehead Reserves to white settlers just before his assassination in 1807. By 1809, it was reported that 201 white families were living here. The Chickasaw Nation protested their presence and by 1810, the U.S. Army had established Fort Hampton near the mouth of Elk River. The mission of the soldiers stationed here was to destroy the crops and burn the homes of these people and push them back across the line into Tennessee.

However, by 1816 a large number of these people had returned to their tomahawk claims. It took the federal government two years following the Treaty of 1816 to survey the land before the sales could commence. Lauderdale County began filling up almost immediately following the first land sale in 1818. The earliest settlements were in the areas of Blue Water Creek near Center Star and Center Hill in the eastern part of the county and Cypress Creek near the community of Huggins which is known now as the Wesley Chapel United Methodist Church Community in the Northwest part of the county.

Florence became the seat of government although its selection was hotly contested by another developer who contended that its location should be closer to the center of the county. The initial court sessions were held in the home of Judge William S.

Fulton, the county's first judge, until the new courthouse was completed in 1822.

The earliest settlers of Lauderdale County were people from Tennessee, Kentucky, Georgia, North and South Carolina, and Virginia. They brought with them strains of ancient cultures, mixed with the local heritage of the Native Americans as well as the African-Americans who came along with the first pioneers. All of these people have left indelible influences on whom we are today.

Signers of Petition to President and Congress
By Intruders on Chickasaw Lands
September 5, 1810

This settlement, known as the Simms settlement, was located in northeast Limestone County near Alabama Highway 127. The two Simms brothers, William and James, were builders of the first cabin there in 1807. According to legend, one of the signers of this petition, Thomas Redus, was allowed to remain so that he could grind corn for the Indians as well as for the white settlers.

Note: This petition was endorsed and addressed to the President of the United States of America, James Madison, by 450 of the Intruders upon the Chickasaw Territory. It was received Oct. 1st, 1810.

Wm Sims	George Brown
James Sims	James Reynolds
Michael Odaniell	Larkin Webb
Thomas Skagg	Isaac Crowson
William Payne	Benjimen Osbourn
Berry Matlock	Robert Cravens

Andrew Arnett	Isaac Mirrell
Jonathan Cohron	Georg Arbuthnot
Hoseph Bradley	Francs Daughty
James Wooley	Bejman Carrel
Henry Lysby	Asa Magge
Isaac Gibson	Sammell Preed Jr.
Samuel Easely	Sammul Preed
David Silmon	James Preed
John Hoddge	Christopher Baylor
John Coward	Marckel Stockden
Charles Skaggs Sen	Thomas Redus
Charles Skaggs Jr.	Richard Murrell
Charles Williams	John Daugherty
William Adams	James Hodges
Wm Bowling Sen	James Hood
Wm Bowling Jr.	William Mayers
Wm Cooper	William Hodges
Wm Conway	William Hoodser
Charles Easely	Edmond Fears
John Scagg	William Hood Jr.
John Eppler	Ely Robertson
James Neill	Samuel Robertson
I Shame Brown	Micel Robertson
Jame Brown	John Allon
Abraham Brown	James Ball
Edward Davis	John McCutchan
Rawleigh Dodson	David McCutchan
Aaron Luisley	John Calwell
Simon Foy	John Bidell
Benj. Murrell	John Rosson
Cavin Wittey	Simon Rosson
Caleb Juett	Richard Linville

Wm. Nelson	William Candon
John Nelson	James Riggs
James Ford	Robert Tayler
James Caldwell	Enoch Tayler
Wm. Kile	John Tayler
Samuel Bradley	Jas Wilder
William Adams	Fracis Ascaugh
Roland McKenny	Joeb Arbagh
James McKenny	Jas Wherrey
John McKenny	John Bell
Ruben McKenny	Benjamin Russell
Robert McKenny	Edward Frost
William McKenny	Jas Anderson
John Lynn	Joseph Evans
Elijah Price	Henry Evans
John Hogges	John Scallorn
John Sessoms	Jacob Scallorn
Amos Moor	John Wain Wright
William Elles	John Myars
John Thomas	James Green
Joshua Perkens	John Mowery
Issac Fraey	Alexander Dutton
Lovill Coffman	George Fergel
Cornelius Gatliff	John Sauls
James Redey	Reel Matcok
John Panton	John Bartell
Jesse Panton	John Kim
William Hooker	Andy Jackson
Thomas Pool	Henry Miller
Philmer Green Sen.	Abraham Miller
Jere McKellens	Robert Foury
Reuben Riggs	Joseph Calvert

Jemes Mossy	Thos Adams
Jemes McMahhan	Robt Wallis
Jessy Cooper	James Isaac
David Miller	Hardin Hulsey
Levi Cummens	William Hill
Mark Mitchens	Jas Miller
Allen Cotton	John Hamlin
John Cottun	Samuel Smith
William Cox	Ellexander Smith
Thomas Hardy	Felps Smith
George Lofen	Wm Smith
John Tayler	Bryan Smith
Lennerd Lofton	Jonathan Greenhow
Joseph Foster	Wm Greenhow
Abraham Kirkelot	Greenbery Greenhow
John Kirkendall	John Croslin
Jos Jones	Benjamin French
Levi Cooper	Henry Croslin
John Cooper	Jessey Richardson
John Paine	Josepph England
Fuller Cox	David Dudden
Saml Cox	John Crage
Joseph Looker	Michal Trimble
William Riggs	Elisha Rainbolt
Bridges Freeman	Jes Craig
Charles Hulsey	John Mitchell Sr.
Beverly Philips	Elisha Garritt
Shaderick Cross	John Mitchell Jr.
Benjamin Ishmal	George Mitchell
Benjn Cross	Wm Smith
Henry Cross	Jno Sanders
Jonathan Adams	Reuben Sanders

Joseph Carnes	Matt Smith
Wm Carnes	James Mullens
Redden Crisp	Jaret Brandon
Wm Black	James Smith
Leml Black	John Miller
Jos Keen	Elijah Major
John Allmen	James Major
Walter Tremble	John Trimble
Elye Hornback	Joshua Brunson
Wm McGowen	David Parkir
Robt Hodgers Jr.	John Ray
Robert Stenson	John Carnham
John Smith	Jacob Pyeatt
John Runnals	James Pyeatt
Francis Bird	Aaron Gibson
Thos Henderson	Cabot Turner
Shadrach Morres	Isack Shipman
Lewis Tacket	John Hakins
William Kellett	George S. Wilson
Joseph Kellett	Josha Bruntson
James Kellett	James Slaughter
James Humphrs	Jesop Luster
William Humphrs	John Luster
Charles Smith	James Luster
William Stephens	Robert McGowen
Samuel Nelson	Danl McIntyre
George Honbre	Alexr Masky
Joel James	John Chambers
Henry Mgain	Thos Price
Wm Mullin	Joel Philips
Thomas Mullin	Wm Stinson
John Toliver	George Hauge

Ezel Smith	Clouds Greenhaw
Wm Smith	Alexander Morr
Andrew Smith	Robert Morr
Jame McConel	John Umphres
Saml McConell	Archable Trimble
James M. McConell	James Garner
William Chambers	John Bell
Jno Webb	James Burlston
George Bankhead	Robert Thresher
Jno Bankhead	David Thompson
Michael Shaly	John Roguey
George Shaly	David Capshaw
Fredrich Shaly	Malachi Reeves
Moses Crosen	Robert Gresham
Moses Chot	Amos French
John Vans	William W. Capshaw
Duncan McAntire	George Ogel
William Voss	George McCrown
Alex Miller	David Allerd
William Cochran	William Magers
John Welch	Harda Allerd
William Welch Sr.	George Cooper
Beverly Luster	David Water
David Luster	John Wager
Jas Bevers	Harmon Horn
Jonathan Burleson	Banra Devon
John Burleson	John Gebbens
Matthew Brunstin	Robt Gebbins
William Slaughter	Saml Gibbons
Jonathan Blair	James Gibbons
John Billensly	Jos Gibbons
Jonathan Greenhaw	Clemen Arman

Mathew Brewer	Thomas Brighton
James Norman	
Aaron Shote	**Names of the Widows:**
John Shote	*Damarias Bowling*
John Wynn	*Amenidab Hattan*
M. Armstrong	*Betsey Williams*
Ths Dodd	*Mehaley Robertson*
Isaac Peritt	*Gilly Crowson*
Jeremiah Rowlen	*Milly Hogwood*
Mitchell O'Neel	*Drankey Medders*
Jessy Dillion	*Patsey Carter*
Tiery O'Neel	*Caty Lewrence*
Hirram O'Neel	*Joan Black*
Joseph Brunson	*Ann Johnstons*
John Parmerly	*Susan Wigges*
Richard Robertson	*Betsey Cooper*
George Taylour	*Ann Grin*
Ellken Taylor	*Elezebith Sims*
John Taylour, Jr.	*Grizell Sims*
Robert Taylour	*Polly Prigman*
Hanum Taylour	*Sally Williams*
John Taylour, Sr.	*Any Taylour*
Thomas Reed	*Christiana MCravay*
John Reed	
Wm Taylour	**Men's Names**
Nathanniel Hannet	Abner Camono
James Dunahoo	Jessey Beavers
James Long	John Hoaton
John Cooper	Nicholess Boren
Leire Cooper	James Boren
James Dunham	Abner Boren
Alexr Dunham	Henry Davis

Benjamin Land	William Cramer
Andrew Blithe	William Murrell
Jacob Blithe	William Smith
Wm Lilly	John Smith
Obediah Martin	John Black, Sr.
Wm Martin	Gabriel Tayour
Henson Day	Nathiniell Harbin
Andrew Pickins	Jessee Harbin
Joseph L. Jones	James Harbin
Hugh Bradon	Robert Wood
Adam Burney	Millenton Tidwell
James Burney	James Leath
Wm Ferrell	Edward Shoat
Owen Shannon	Vantenten Shoat
William Cooper	John Taylour
Jas Braden	Benjamin Tutt
James Steward	James Pickins
John Cooper	
Levi Cooper	
Chale Dever	
John Black, Jr.	
Prier Kile	
Rcuben Smith	
Isac Lann	
Eli Tidwell	
Millin Tidwell	
Eli Tidwell	
Daniel Kinny	
Owin Shannon, Sr.	
James Renn	
H. T. Hendry	
Jos L. Hendry	

Index

Brown, Abraham · 170
Brown, George · 169
Brown, I Shame · 170
Brown, Jame · 170
Brown, James · 166
Brown, John · 124
Brown, Jos · 166
Brunson, Joseph · 175
Brunson, Joshua · 173
Brunstin, Matthew · 174
Bruntson, Josha · 173
Buckner, Phillip · 45
Bullen, Joseph · 42, 44
Bulls, Will · 155
Burleson, John · 174
Burleson, Jonathan · 174
Burlston, James · 174
Burner, Wm · 164
Burnett · 68
Burney · 74
Burney, Adam · 176
Burney, C. L. · 166
Burney, Charles L. · 166
Burney, James · 176
Burney, John W. · 166
Burney, Samuel, Jr. · 166
Burney, Samuel, Sr. · 165, 167
Burney, W. W. · 166
Burney, Wm · 163
Butler · 74
Butler, Gabriel · 137, 138, 139, 164, 166
Butler, John · 137, 164, 166
Butler, Kit · 78
Butler, Richard · 137, 164
Butler, Richd · 166
Butler, T. · 166
Butler, Thomas · 137, 163, 164

C

Caldwell, James · 171
Calvert, Joseph · 171
Calwell, John · 170
Camono, Abner · 175
Campbel, Alexander · 166
Campbell · 142
Campbell, Alexander · 142

Campbell, Gustavus · 142
Campbell, John · 142
Campbell, Peter · 142
Campbell, Robert · 142
Campbell, Solomon · 142
Campbell, William · 142
Candon, William · 171
Caplin, Thomas · 166
Capshaw, David · 174
Capshaw, William W. · 174
Carnes, Joseph · 173
Carnes, Wm · 173
Carnham, John · 173
Carrel, Alexander · 166
Carrel, Bejman · 170
Carter, Kilpatrick · 40
Carter, Patsey · 175
Carwood, W. · 166
Casey, Nathaniel · 166
Casey, Thomas · 166
Cassity, Levi · 80, 86
Cavenner, John · 166
Chambers, Jno · 165
Chambers, John · 173
Chambers, William · 174
Chealty · 33
Checkout · 74
Cherokee · 17, 20, 26, 27, 28, 29, 30, 35, 49, 53, 64, 66, 67, 68, 72, 73, 76, 78, 80, 81, 82, 84, 85, 92, 95, 98, 99, 103, 105, 107, 110, 111, 115, 116, 119, 120, 121, 122, 123, 124, 125, 127, 129, 131, 138, 146, 147, 148, 152, 155, 157, 159, 160, 162, 163, 167, 168
Chickamaugas · 110, 111, 112
Chickasaw · iv, 13, 17, 18, 20, 21, 27, 29, 30, 31, 32, 33, 35, 38, 39, 40, 41, 42, 43, 45, 48, 49, 51, 52, 53, 54, 55, 56, 57, 59, 60, 66, 68, 81, 93, 95, 98, 99, 103, 105, 106, 107, 108, 109, 110, 112, 113, 119, 120, 121, 122, 125, 126, 127, 134, 135, 138, 140, 144, 146, 155, 159, 160, 161, 167, 168, 169
Chickemicaws · 21

2

9

11

Published by

Bluewater Publications is a multi-faceted publishing company capable of meeting all of your reading and publishing needs. Our two-fold aim is to:

1) Provide the market with educationally enlightening and inspiring research and reading materials and to
2) Make the opportunity of being published available to any author and or researcher who so desires to become published.

We are passionate about preserving history; whether it is through the re-publishing of an out-of-print classic or by publishing the research of historians and genealogists, Bluewater Publications is the publisher you need.

To learn more about Dr. McDonald or for information about how you can be published through Bluewater Publications, please visit:

www.BluewaterPublications.com

Confidently Preserving Our Past,
Angela Broyles and Crystal Broyles
Bluewater Publications.com
Formerly Known as Heart of Dixie Publishing